Petticoat Politics

Petticoat Politics

HOW AMERICAN WOMEN WON THE RIGHT TO VOTE

★ ★ ★ ★ ★ ★ ★ ★ ★ ★ ★ ★ ★ ★ ★ ★ ★

by Doris Faber

Lothrop, Lee & Shepard Co., Inc.
NEW YORK

The author is grateful to the H. W. Wilson Company for permission to quote from Mary Gray Peck's Carrie Chapman Catt, *which it published in 1944. Permission has also been obtained from the Beacon Press to quote from* Front Door Lobby, *copyright © 1960 by Edna Lamprey Stantial.*

Contents

An Opening Note

═══════════

A cry of protest has stirred the United States during recent years. With mounting intensity, a whole century after the Civil War, voices everywhere have been demanding the full rights of citizenship for Americans whose skins happen to be dark. In the short memory of some, it has seemed this campaign is something new in American history, but that is not so. Just half a century ago, the streets of our cities and towns rang out with similar demonstrations, and the cause then was similar, too. Those earlier voices were demanding the full rights of citizenship for Americans who happened to be born female.

It is difficult for the present generation of young Americans to realize how hard some of their grandmothers had to fight before winning the right to vote. Indeed the great-grand-mothers, and even the great-great-grandmothers of some, began the fight. At that time, women had almost no legal rights; if they happened to earn any money, it belonged to their husbands; if their husbands beat them, that was too bad, but the law would not interfere. Although the great majority of American women probably were treated kindly, still men

were by law their lords and masters. The parallel between the
status of women then and the status of Negro slaves was certainly not exact. But it was close enough for the spirited
women who began the feminist reform movement to cry out
against the enslavement of their sex—and to demand emancipation.

How these women fought, what obstacles blocked their
way for the better part of a century—this is the story to be
told in the pages that follow. From the personal memoirs of
the participants in the struggle, from old newspapers and
scrapbooks, have come the raw materials for constructing the
narrative.

A fuller discussion of sources will be found with the
bibliography at the back of the book, but I would like to
take this opportunity to thank those who helped me in my research at the New York Public Library, the New York Historical Society, and the New York Society Library; the Library of Congress; and the Schlesinger Library of Radcliffe
College (formerly known as the Women's Archives). I must
also thank various officials of the League of Women Voters;
Dr. Louise Young of American University; and several former
colleagues at the *New York Times* for steering me toward
valuable material.

In a sense, this book has been in the making ever since
1948, when as a young reporter I covered a series of events in
Seneca Falls and Rochester, New York, commemorating the
one hundredth anniversary of the first woman's rights convention. Grandnieces and granddaughters of some of the 1848
participants were on hand then, gracing ceremonies that
seemed at the time delightfully quaint but hardly very mean-
ingful in the modern world. But the civil rights struggle of
the 1960's has put the feminist movement in a new perspec-
tive. I hope the pages that follow will amply demonstrate this.

D.F.

Half
a Pair
of
Scissors?

1

Neat rows of red brick houses faced each other. This was
Philadelphia in the 1830's, and a cart rumbled across the
cobbled roadway. The cry of a street vendor rang out, offering the city's favorite steaming, spicy stew of meat and vege-
tables: "Pepper POT! Smoking HOT!"

But within doors, the street sounds were muffled. Guests
sitting at the long dining table presided over by a sweet-faced
woman in Quaker gray were much too absorbed to heed any
such distractions. Throughout the meal, the conversation had
been lively.

Was not Thomas Jefferson quite as worthy of political
reverence as George Washington himself? While soup was
being served from a seemingly bottomless tureen, this topic,
introduced by the handsome, broad-shouldered host, occupied
not only the gentlemen but the ladies, too.

Did Shakespeare in truth write all of the plays credited to
him, or did other poets write several? During the carving of
the roast, the attention of the company was directed to this
subject by a visitor from Connecticut, a lady who had recently
founded a seminary for the higher education of girls. En-

lightened though she was in regard to developing female intellect, she may have felt it not entirely fitting for females to discuss political questions.

Whatever her views, however, the company as a whole did not hold with ordinary notions of propriety. This was proved as the meal drew toward a close.

Then a young serving maid entered, carrying a well-scrubbed little cedar tub filled with steaming water, and she placed it on the table in front of her mistress. Guests dining here for the first time may have been somewhat surprised, but except for a friendly smile or two, no other notice was taken as Mrs. Lucretia Mott began a task more usually performed elsewhere. While her company continued its spirited conversation, she calmly washed and dried the dishes.

It was like Lucretia Mott to deal thus sensibly, if unconventionally, with household problems. Although her husband seemed on the road to prospering as a wool merchant, luxurious living went against her principles. On the other hand, she had no mind to keep visitors away from her door, or to admit them, serve them, and then disappear herself to some mysterious backstairs region, thereby missing any stimulating discussion. Surely not!

Despite her gentle manner she was no mere listener either. During the past ten years, ever since the death of her first-born boy had turned her mind strongly to religion, she had been "in the preaching line," as her father proudly put it. The Quaker faith had a long tradition of allowing women to speak at meeting. But Mrs. Mott did not confine her speaking out to Sunday meeting, or to matters of religious doctrine. More and more, she was becoming convinced that she had a duty to plead another cause in season and out of season.

"Move up—come forward!" Mrs. Mott urged as soon as she had finished the dishes and led her company into the parlor. "Do come more into a circle!" On the round table in front of the fireplace, beside her own chair, there was a book; but she did not refer to it—yet. Instead, in her singularly clear voice, she proceeded, as she did almost daily, to seek new friends for the cause of the downtrodden slave.

"The millions of slaves in our land form our most oppressed class," Lucretia Mott would say time after time. "I feel bound to do all in my power, in every right effort for their immediate emancipation." Then she would tell of the program of Mr. Garrison of Boston, who was planning to hold a convention in Philadelphia of like-minded people willing to establish an American Anti-Slavery Society; would her listeners not find it within their hearts to join this movement?

Among the thoughtful men and women who gathered in Mrs. Mott's parlor there were always some who raised objections. William Lloyd Garrison's own words antagonized many: "I WILL BE HEARD!" he wrote belligerently in his paper, the *Liberator,* and every week he hurled new angry tirades that could only stiffen the resistance of Southern slaveowners; was this a "right effort"? Would it not be wiser to look for a less radical leader, with a more gradual program? And . . . considering that there were ladies present, was it suitable for ladies even to think of enlisting in a political sort of movement?

Slavery was, above all, a moral problem, Mrs. Mott would reply, and Mr. Garrison was a moral leader, not a politician. Having entertained him in her own home, she could also add that he was far milder in his manner personally than might be expected from the tone of his writings; and his tone could be excused on the ground that forceful leadership was needed to arouse the nation about the evil of slavery. As to the suitability of women taking part in such a crusade, Mrs. Mott would reach for the book on her small round table.

Vindication of the Rights of Woman, it was called. Some forty years back, in 1792, a woman named Mary Wollstonecraft had written the book in London. Her daughter was the Mary Wollstonecraft Shelley who had written the novel *Frankenstein,* and had married the English poet, Percy Shelley.

As for herself, Mrs. Mott would remark, she rarely had time to read poetry or novels; however, this essay by the original Mary Wollstonecraft deserved a most thorough reading. Anyone wondering whether women had the right to work for the anti-slavery cause, or any other cause in which they sincerely believed, could find ample support for an affirmative answer in this volume, Mrs. Mott would suggest—and offer to lend her copy to any friend present.

Serenely smiling, she would assure her guests that she herself came by her outspoken spirit naturally. On the island of Nantucket up in Massachusetts, where she had been born on January 3, 1793, into an old Quaker family, the women learned self-reliance of necessity. While the menfolk were off on their whaling ships for months at a time, their wives kept penny shops to help support their households, and ran farms or even other businesses. These women were a level-headed group. "They were not triflers," Mrs. Mott would observe. "They had intelligent subjects of conversation."

Indeed she was always pleased to recall that one of her early feminine forebears had, in effect, governed the island for many years. Of course it would have been unthinkable that a woman should seek public office, yet there was no doubt of her great-great-grandaunt's superior common sense. Thus a system had evolved that did no violence to accepted opinion, and still gave the community the benefit of Aunt Mary's wisdom. At every town meeting, Aunt Mary would settle disputed issues merely by rising and tactfully saying: *"My husband* thinks that . . ."

Now, more than a century later, the prevailing opinion on the matter of woman's proper sphere had not changed. It remained unthinkable that a woman might take any open part in politics or governmental affairs; even to display an interest in such questions was considered unladylike. As Mrs. Mott was only too well aware, her own activities on behalf of the poor of the city and now on behalf of the slave—her preaching and now her organizing—were in some quarters considered dangerously wrong. Home and family were supposed to be the limits beyond which feminine minds must not venture, and strong walls of law and custom prevented all but the boldest from defying the established order.

Certainly the settled nature of the prevailing system seemed secure against any serious upheaval. In the energetic young United States, as in the Old World, married women were effectively limited from embarking on any major independent action. They could not own property of any description, whether an inheritance from their own relatives or even money they might earn themselves; their husbands had full legal control of every penny. Married women could not sign any official document; their husbands had to sign for them. Married women had no right under law to protect their children; even a notorious drunkard had unquestioned sway over his children, and in the event that a wife defied custom by leaving such a man, the law said she had to leave her children, too.

The case of women who did not marry was still harder in many ways. Teaching young children was almost the only respectable work by which they could earn their living; other professions and trades were effectively closed by the fact that advanced schooling was almost universally denied to females. And the pay offered to female teachers in the primary grades was usually a mere pittance—half, or less than half, of what a male teacher would command, as Lucretia Mott herself had discovered to her distress when she taught briefly at the Quaker school where a tall, solemn, blond young man named James Mott was an instructor in the boys' division.

James Mott shared his wife's convictions about right and wrong and encouraged her to speak out; James, like Lucretia, came to believe freedom for Negro slaves was imperative; and James supported Lucretia when she reached the conclusion that the time had come for women, too, to be emancipated. Thus, James and Lucretia's sedate dinner parties were one of the earliest and most significant stirrings in what was to become a great social upheaval.

Had Lucretia Mott been less womanly and more fiery, she could not have accomplished all she did. A few other women, like the flamboyant Frances Wright, who inherited a small fortune in Scotland and spent it traipsing across the United States spouting feminism in the 1830's, were ridiculed mercilessly for their personal quirks, and did their cause little good. Margaret Fuller from Boston wrote brilliantly on the subject a decade later, but was laughed at as a freakish spinster—until she caused even more sarcastic comment by upping at the age of thirty-seven and marrying a young Italian count in Rome. But Lucretia Mott, in her starched Quaker bonnet, demurely sewing rags into carpet squares in the snug comfort of her front parlor, unmistakably a devoted wife and mother, could not be so rudely dismissed. When she earnestly recommended Mary Wollstonecraft's book, this defense of woman's rights not only turned up on tea tables in Philadelphia; copies were also sent to married sisters in New York State and Ohio, till the book became a sort of bible among educated women.

Yet the printed word, no matter how fervently written and then fervently discussed, would not of itself have started any revolution. The Wollstonecraft book had already been available for forty years without causing feminist armies to rise. Other conditions had to be ripe before something happened.

The Industrial Revolution had to reach the stage where cities were growing, leisure for middle-class women was increasing, and all manner of new ideas were being explored. Then, inevitably, reform movements of every conceivable variety began flourishing. From the two reform movements of widest appeal in the United States—the temperance campaign to restrict the use of alcoholic beverages, and the militant abolitionist campaign to end slavery—the woman's rights struggle emerged.

"We have good cause to be grateful to the slave," said Abby Kelley, a sharp-tongued lady from Massachusetts. "In striving to strike his irons off, we found most surely that *we* were manacled *ourselves.*"

When women moved beyond their own firesides, to attend rallies, to listen as resolutions were introduced and discussed, many of them felt an impulse to do more than listen. Why not speak up, too? Arranging cake and needlework sales to raise money for the cause was all very well, and indeed it provided needed experience in organizing, in hiring a hall, in working on committees. Yet why must women, merely because they were women, remain silent when important policy questions were being decided?

Discovering no satisfactory answer, some women did begin rising to their feet in public. Shocked murmurs swept around them; pious clergymen tried to hush them. Then intelligent women started flocking into the feminist camp, and natural leaders like Lucretia Mott found themselves all but forced to make woman's rights their main cause.

Mrs. Mott was not the only figure who gained renown during the early days of this struggle. For a time, two startling young ladies from South Carolina, the Grimké sisters, were more famous, because it was they who provoked the first big controversy about the proper role of women.

Daughters of a wealthy plantation owner, Angelina and Sarah Grimké both detested slavery and had quit the South when they inherited some money. Angelina was handsome, Sarah was plain; but they both felt the same call, once they had come North, to tell their firsthand knowledge of how evil slavery was, and by 1835 they were speaking regularly under the auspices of various anti-slavery societies.

At the beginning, the sisters spoke only before groups of ladies gathered in the parlors of private homes. But Angelina was reputed to be so unusually pretty, yet so marvelously eloquent, that quite some curiosity developed whenever a Grimké lecture was scheduled. Soon the demand for invitations was such that halls were being hired; still, to preserve decorum, only ladies were supposed to attend. However, one or two husbands had the notion of coming along with their wives to view Angelina's fine dark eyes for themselves. Despite the prevailing opinion that it was the height of immodesty for women to address mixed audiences, more and more men kept appearing to hear the Grimkés, until the polite fiction that their lectures were for ladies only had to be abandoned. In the Boston Opera House, Angelina and Sarah spoke several times before some of the largest audiences ever assembled in that city.

Then came an ominous rumbling. The Council of Congregationalist Ministers of Massachusetts, representing the largest religious group in the state, met in 1836 to consider what must be done. The result of their meeting was a letter denouncing unwomanly behavior in no uncertain terms, and an order that the letter be read from every Congregationalist pulpit the following Sunday:

"We invite your attention to the dangers which at present

threaten the female character with widespread and permanent injury. . . ."

On for several ponderous paragraphs, the ministers preached that woman's true mission, as set forth in holy writings, was solely that of wife and mother; that she was, and must always be, subordinate to man; that any interference with this natural order must be viewed as having most serious consequences to the stability of the family and all human society. In a flourish of poetic imagery, they concluded:

"If the vine, whose strength and beauty is to lean upon the trellis-work, thinks to assume the independence and overshadowing nature of the elm, it will not only cease to bear fruit, but fall in shame and dishonor into the dust."

Sarah Grimké, a more polished writer than her sister, immediately took on the task of replying to this attack, in a lengthy and closely reasoned sermon of her own. After proving her erudition by quoting from religious writings supporting a wider role for woman, she concluded: "To me, it is perfectly clear that *whatsoever it is morally right for a man to do, it is morally right for a woman to do.*"

Despite the urgings of many men with whom they had been working on the anti-slavery cause, both sisters refused to forget the woman's rights issue and concentrate on slavery. Sarah spent much of her time writing articles, and then a widely circulated book, on the subject. But it was the lovely Angelina who put the reason for their change in emphasis most persuasively, in a letter to the abolitionist leader Theodore Weld who, in turn, convinced her to marry him two years later.

"*We* cannot push Abolitionism forward with all our might," Angelina wrote to him, "*until* we take up the stumbling block out of the road. You may depend upon it, tho' to meet *this* question *may appear* to be turning out of our road, that *it is not*. IT IS NOT: we *must* meet it and meet it now. . . . If we surrender the right to *speak* in public this year, we must surrender the right to petition next year, and the right to *write* the year after, and so on. What *then* can *woman* do for the slave, when she herself is under the feet of man and shamed into *silence?"*

What indeed? Back in Philadelphia, Lucretia Mott was finding it necessary to ponder the same question. In 1833 she did help Mr. Garrison form the American Anti-Slavery Society; already well-known as a speaker at Quaker meetings, she did dare to rise at the organizing meeting of the abolitionist group. After humbly apologizing for intruding her own views, she had suggested a change in the wording of a resolution—and she caused at least one minister to modify his previous convictions.

"I had never before heard a woman speak at a public meeting," he said afterward. "She said but a few words, but these were spoken so modestly, in such sweet tones, and yet withal so decisively, that no one could fail to be pleased."

Nevertheless, even in the case of Lucretia Mott, there were some who failed to be pleased by what appeared to them a bold flaunting of the proprieties. In deference to such opinion, it seemed wise to form separate women's anti-slavery societies. The ladies could meet on their own, speak on their own, even send out petitions of their own, without offensively competing with men. Mrs. Mott herself accepted this view for a few years.

Yet the women alone did not succeed in accomplishing very much. If she thought she had begun to understand why, Mrs. Mott became sure of the reason when she received a letter from Mrs. Lydia Maria Child, who was prominent in Boston abolitionist circles. Mrs. Mott had written to invite Mrs.

Lucretia Mott.

Child to come to Philadelphia as a delegate to a proposed convention of female anti-slavery societies. With good humor but decisively, Mrs. Child declined, saying:

"I have never entered very earnestly into the plan of female societies. They always seemed to me like half a pair of scissors. . . ."

Half a pair of scissors? With a sewing basket almost constantly beside her, Mrs. Mott had to smile at the suggestion. Why, every woman knew that half a pair of scissors could not possibly cut a single thread!

To end the evil of slavery, it would take the best efforts of every dedicated person, man and woman, working together, and the road ahead would not be easy. People had to be persuaded that the issue was urgent. Ever since militant abolition groups had started insisting on action, numerous respectable citizens had become angered at being forced to face an unpleasant question, and rougher elements had become more than angry. Up in Boston, Mr. Garrison had been dragged out of a meeting by a rope tied around his waist, and if protection had not been forthcoming, the horror of a hanging might even have occurred. In Philadelphia itself, hoodlums had burned the hall where an abolitionist convention was to assemble, then stormed through the streets looking for abolitionists to stone.

"On to Motts'!" the mob had even shouted. Having sent their younger children to a neighbor's house for safety, Lucretia and James had sat, calmly waiting in their own parlor.

That mob had spent its fury without doing more than threaten, but what might the future hold? Lucretia Mott knew some would consider it only prudent to cease speaking out against slavery, yet she never seriously thought of any such prudence. Instead she expanded her activities on behalf of the emancipation of all Negro slaves.

By doing so, she also took the step that would lead in a direct line to the emancipation of women. Up until this time, nobody had seriously proposed that the most significant symbol of full citizenship—the right to vote—should belong to women, as well as men. Lucretia Mott herself had never for an instant entertained so radical an idea. But when she stepped aboard a ship in New York harbor in the spring of 1840, on her way to attend a world anti-slavery congress in London, she was bringing the ballot closer for all of the women of the world.

Behind
the Bar

2

Despite the bright spring sunshine, Lucretia Mott found the bricks of London rough and black, compared with Philadelphia. Like many a visitor before and after her, she wondered at the English custom she noted, and described in her diary, of "tea always made at table . . . dry toast always in a rack." But she was warmed constantly by the friendly welcome she met everywhere, except in the preliminary councils of the great congress she had come to attend.

"*Gentlemen only are expected to attend.*" The smug words made her shiver with fresh indignation each time she heard them. And during the few days remaining before the congress officially convened, she heard them repeatedly from the lips of clergymen, of members of Parliament, and other respected leaders in the British anti-slavery movement who had taken the initiative in calling this international conclave. The words were spoken politely, even with deference, and they were often followed by the most courteous expressions of regret. Nevertheless, the main point could not be missed.

Women delegates were to be denied any voice in the deliberations. A dozen ladies had come all the way from America because they had been selected to represent active anti-slavery societies; there could be no doubt of their loyalty to the abolition cause, no defect of any reasonable sort stood in their way. The only trouble was a matter over which nobody had any control. They had been born female.

But this absurd restriction was to be challenged!

As the acknowledged leader of the feminine contingent, Lucretia Mott was well aware of the difficulties ahead. Even before setting sail, she had known what to anticipate. "I am sure the kindest thing," one of the English sponsors of the congress had written to Mr. Garrison about the American women delegates, "I am sure the kindest thing to them, as well as the best for our cause, would be for you to do all you can to discourage them."

But discouraging the ladies was no part of Mr. Garrison's purpose. Already he had proved himself the staunchest friend the women abolitionists had; by insisting on placing the tart Abby Kelley among the directors of his American Anti-Slavery Society, he had forced an open split in the whole abolition movement in the United States. Diverging views about politics would probably have split the movement soon enough anyhow, but those who disagreed on political matters also tended to disagree on the place of women, and after a heated debate in New York about whether Abby Kelley should be raised to the eminence proposed for her, the American abolition movement had separated into two camps.

Now Mr. Garrison led the camp that held women entitled to full equality with men in anti-slavery councils. It was his group that had chosen to send Lucretia Mott to London; and various female anti-slavery societies affiliated with this parent body had chosen the other feminine delegates. Rather than discourage the ladies, Mr. Garrison aimed to fight for them.

The opposition was bound to be furious. Conservative old England seemed to be prospering under the rule of young Queen Victoria, who had ascended the throne just three years earlier, in 1837; but it appeared that an important segment of British opinion would be outraged at the thought of lesser women taking part in public debate. Furthermore, many of the American delegates represented the anti-feminist camp, and no doubt hoped for revenge after having suffered the indignity of being obliged to listen to women speakers on their own side of the ocean.

But did these two groups truly account for a majority of the delegates? Lucretia Mott devoutly hoped not. In any case, the question would not stay unanswered, because to her great satisfaction, a test on the issue was being planned by a group of sympathetic men.

Unfortunately, Mr. Garrison himself had not yet arrived in London, his ship having been delayed. Nevertheless, the imposing Wendell Phillips of Boston, the best orator in the abolition movement, had agreed to lead the fight on behalf of the women. Assisting Mr. Phillips would be a goodly number of men from the Massachusetts and Pennsylvania delegations.

All of these were residing in a comfortable old hotel on Great Queen Street while awaiting the formal opening of the congress on the twelfth of June. With her husband, who had accompanied her, Lucretia Mott was part of the same company, as were the other women delegates. In addition, some from the anti-Garrison camp had also taken lodgings in the same establishment, being still friendly with their former associates even if matters of principle now separated them.

Among the "new group," as the secessionists liked to refer to themselves, was a gentleman from New York with journalistic ambitions. Henry B. Stanton had come to London to attend the anti-slavery congress, to write home about it, and for a personal reason, too. Only a few days before sailing, he had married a spirited young lady from upper New York State, and the trip was their honeymoon. In the entire history of the struggle for woman's rights, probably no other single happening was of more significance than the meeting of Lucretia Mott and this bright-eyed bride.

The new Mrs. Stanton had been Miss Elizabeth Cady— "Lizzie" to all of her friends. She was the daughter of a judge who had tried to bring her up as a proper, dutiful female, and despite many an inner struggle, on the whole she had behaved satisfactorily. Then, while visiting some cousins, she had met a man of whom her father could not approve; at the age of twenty-five, she had run away to marry her Henry.

Henry Stanton was no wild-eyed abolitionist, but he did speak and write most effectively for the cause; that was the basis of Judge Cady's disapproval. The judge would have much preferred a more respectable sort of son-in-law, who would practice law in the small town near Albany where the Cadys were leading citizens, and would perhaps follow in his own footsteps to the House of Representatives in Washington. Had Judge Cady foreseen the path on which marriage would take his Elizabeth, doubtless his distress would have been infinitely more painful.

For almost as soon as she declared her independence by marrying her own choice, Elizabeth found the cause she had been yearning for all her life. She found it when she met Lucretia Mott in London.

Even on shipboard, the new Mrs. Stanton had showed a certain freedom that disturbed a fellow passenger quite like her own father in outlook. When this gentleman seemed clearly upset by her behavior at dinner, she playfully asked him to help her and tell her what she was doing wrong. In her diary, she noted down his answer: "I heard you call your husband 'Henry' in the presence of strangers, which is not permissible in polite society. You should always say 'Mr. Stanton.'"

This gentleman's reaction to Lizzie in London can only be imagined. Then she defied polite society on a far more serious point. In London, she learned that through her marriage she had "inherited" a set of opinions she could not agree with; she was embarrassed, and she decisively acted.

For Lizzie had fallen in love with a man whose convictions made him what was then called a political abolitionist; this meant that he favored hard campaigning to elect specific anti-slavery candidates for public office, a position Mr. Garrison scorned. The Garrison wing of the American abolition movement insisted that descending to party politics would darken the high moral climate of their crusade. Having broken with Mr. Garrison on the political issue, Henry Stanton belonged, of necessity, in the opposite camp. Thus he was supposed to be against women delegates—and so was his wife.

Sailing across the Atlantic, Lizzie had gathered only a limited view of the controversy. In the opinion of her husband's friends, it was more than regrettable that some women were fanning the flames of dissension in anti-slavery ranks; being unfamiliar with any of the details of the dispute, she tended to accept what she was told, as a good wife should. But when she arrived at Great Queen Street, and found herself the only female associated with the anti-Garrison faction, she immediately began to wonder.

She sensed at once that the other ladies were hostile to her, all except the gentle Mrs. Mott, who received her with cordiality and courtesy. Approaching the age of fifty now, more than old enough to be Lizzie's mother, Mrs. Mott appeared maternally touched by the alert little bride with such curly black hair and sparkling blue eyes, and even seated the newcomer by her side at dinner.

The moment the large group had settled at a long table, several Baptist ministers began to rally the ladies at not having been satisfied with setting abolitionists by the ears in America. There was a distinct cutting edge to their words as they went on to charge the ladies with proposing to do the same thing now in England.

So woman's rights was to be the big issue here! As Lizzie grasped the fact, she murmured aloud, which could not but endear her to Mrs. Mott. For the moment, though, Lizzie was much too busy inwardly bemoaning her own position to notice anything else, even her husband's uneasy glances at her.

Then as Mrs. Mott calmly and skillfully parried the clergymen's thrusts, Lizzie quite forgot her own awkward situation. She forgot it to the extent that, after a particularly sneering comment from one of the men—despite several warning nudges under the table by Henry—she herself spoke up boldly for her sex.

"I shall never forget," Elizabeth Cady Stanton wrote later, "the look of recognition Mrs. Mott gave me when she saw, by my remarks, that I comprehended the problem of woman's rights and wrongs. How beautiful she looked to me that day."

From this sudden, unspoken sympathy between two women so different in age and background, yet so similar in their independence of spirit, there emerged the revolutionary woman's rights movement.

The prologue to that world-shaking drama came only a few days later, on the date set for the formal opening of the international anti-slavery congress. Then all of the gentlemen—and ladies—temporarily residing on Great Queen Street made their way through the crooked streets of London to Freemason's Hall on Drury Lane. Brilliant sunshine dappled the old city with light and shadow; it was an apt setting for the scene about to unfold.

Outside the nobly proportioned hall, one of the largest in London, streams of delegates from numerous lands were converging. As befitting the host country and the one which had already showed the way by freeing all slaves in its West Indian domains, Britain's contingent was the biggest. A scattering of earnest men representing various distant nations also was in evidence, but the only other major delegation belonged to the United States. And it was this group which drew the main attention.

What was to be done about the American ladies? The buzz of alarm that greeted their appearance left no doubt that this question had captured the lion's share of interest, Lizzie Stanton wryly told herself. Yet the answer was not to be long in forthcoming. Even as new little knots of gesturing delegates kept forming, polite ushers began leading the way toward the seats filling the main body of the hall. Male delegates, that is, were thus ceremoniously escorted; the American females were led with equal politeness to a separate area opposite the entrance. There, in a section set apart by a metal bar upon which a curtain hung, they were to be allowed to listen to the proceedings while decently hidden from view— to listen, but not to participate.

The ladies were not surprised; the informal preliminary discussions on Great Queen Street had clearly established this as the procedure to be expected. Nevertheless, all of the ladies wore an air of eager anticipation. Excepting Lizzie Stanton, they were a sensible-looking group in their middle years or older, mainly garbed in modest Quaker gray. Yet even the most grandmotherly gave the impression of being as excited as a girl.

For they still had high hopes. Despite the bar and its curtain, they knew their presence was not to be ignored. Indeed no sooner had the formalities of calling the assemblage to order been completed, than Mr. Phillips of Boston rose and a stir swept through the hall. It was not only the ladies who had advance knowledge that something extraordinary was about to occur.

Mr. Phillips was a true gentleman, recognized as one of the ornaments of the abolition movement. A fine figure of a man, as easy in his manner as any member of the House of Lords, he effortlessly gave the lie to those who sneered that abolitionists were an unwashed lot. Above the rim of the curtain, he appeared to Lizzie Stanton almost majestic as he stood to introduce a motion.

"Resolved," he started in his splendid, ringing voice, "resolved that a committee of five be appointed to prepare a *correct list* of the members of this convention . . ." He paused, allowing the import of his words to be appreciated, ". . . with instructions to include in such list," he continued, *"all persons* bearing credentials from any anti-slavery body."

All persons! Could his meaning be clearer? Here was an unmistakable challenge to those who opposed the ladies.

Instantly half a dozen men rose to their feet, among them a known partisan of the "new group" in American abolitionism. Surely this gentleman could be counted on to counter Mr. Phillips most effectively. Those who thought so, however, had failed to consider the persuasive powers of a certain blue-eyed bride.

For the stocky, energetic Mr. Stanton of New York astonished many in the assemblage when he proceeded to deliver an eloquent plea—in favor of admitting women delegates to full membership in the convention. Disconcerted, but far from ready to concede defeat, others committed to the exclusion of the women jumped to their feet. The debate was on!

THE REVEREND HENRY GREW OF PHILADELPHIA: The reception of women as a part of this convention would, in the view of many, be not only a violation of the customs of England, but of the ordinance of Almighty God. . . .

GEORGE BRADBURN OF MASSACHUSETTS: We are told that it would be outraging the customs of England to allow women to sit in this convention. I have a great respect for the customs of old England. But I ask, gentlemen, if it be right to set up the customs and habits, not to say prejudices of Englishmen, as a standard for the government on this occasion of Americans. . . .

CAPTAIN WANCHOPE OF THE ROYAL NAVY: I entreat the ladies not to push this question too far. . . .

THE REVEREND DR. MORRISON: I believe that we are treading on the brink of a precipice. . . .

At last, the hour being late, the chairman called for a vote, and then there could no longer be any doubt. By an overwhelming majority, the male delegates voted to exclude women from any participation in the convention.

When the stir caused by the tally subsided, the British chairman asked that Mr. Phillips of Boston rise once more. "I hope, as the question is now decided," said this gentleman, "that Mr. Phillips will give us the assurance that we shall proceed with one heart and one mind."

Peering over the curtain, Lizzie Stanton waited confidently. Certainly Mr. Phillips would do no such thing; he was bound to defend the rights of women with no less vigor than he would spend defending freedom for Negro slaves. But Mr. Phillips apparently saw a distinction that eluded her.

"There is no unpleasant feeling in our minds," Wendell Phillips said smoothly. *"I have no doubt the women will sit with as much interest behind the bar* as though the original proposition had been carried in the affirmative. All we asked was an expression of opinion, and, having obtained it, we shall now act with the utmost cordiality."

So Mr. Phillips was quite satisfied! But Lizzie Stanton was not. Never in her long life would she forget the mortifying moment when she listened to this bland surrender of the rights of Mrs. Mott and the other dedicated Quaker ladies in the American delegation.

"This assemblage of philanthropists," she wrote sarcastically about the men delegates, "would have been horrified at the idea of burning the flesh of the distinguished women present with red-hot irons, but the crucifixion of their pride and self-respect, the humiliation of their spirit, seemed to them a trifling matter. . . ."

Not for some years would Elizabeth Cady Stanton write these words, but on the evening when the humiliation she mentioned was only minutes old, she and Lucretia Mott left Freemason's Hall in London, walking arm in arm.

"It's time," Lizzie Stanton told Mrs. Mott that evening, "it's time some demand is made for new liberties for women."

"Why, Lizzie, Thee Will Make Us Ridiculous!"

3

Lizzie Stanton was eight years older and the mother of five lively young boys before circumstances made it possible for her and Mrs. Mott to act upon the resolve they had taken in London—and call a woman's rights convention.

The years had been kind to Mrs. Stanton; although she was plumper, and her black hair already had strands of gray, she still had the bright eyes of a girl, along with her appealing air of being so interested in every new sight and sound that other people were magnetically drawn to her. But alas, in the upper New York village where she and her husband had finally settled down, there were all too few diversions for her active mind.

As to keeping busy, she had more than enough to do looking after her brood of boys. The eldest, named for his father, already considered himself an inventor, and delighted in such experiments as making a life preserver of corks and testing its virtues by dropping his eighteen-month-old brother into the Seneca River, naked, with corks tied under his arms.

In the interests of science, the young Henry, stationed in a rowboat, patiently watched the baby splashing; accustomed to a daily bath in a large tub, the little one paddled away quite happily, but he was cold and blue when finally rescued by his mother. Then the very next day, the same infant was seen by a passing stranger, climbing up the highest peak of the Stanton roof. No sooner had Mrs. Stanton once more hurried to the rescue, when she discovered that her three oldest boys had conspired to lock the fourth in the smoke-house. After he was freed, the three offenders were imprisoned in an attic with two barred windows. They kicked out the bars, slid down the lightning rod, and made for the barn to consider fresh mischief.

"This is a fair sample of the quiet happiness I enjoy in the first years of motherhood," Mrs. Stanton wrote to a friend.

Nevertheless, she did thoroughly enjoy her family, and for a few years, child-tending absorbed all of her energy. These were the years immediately after returning from Europe, when she and her husband had made peace with Judge Cady, even coming to live up in Johnstown while the once-scorned son-in-law dutifully studied legal lore. Then there had been an exciting spell in Boston, where Henry Stanton thought to set up a law practice and Elizabeth eagerly attended lectures by Mr. Emerson. But this move proved financially disastrous, so the Stantons moved once more, to the New York village of Seneca Falls, in which there was an old house a client of Judge Cady's made available at a most reasonable rental.

Lizzie Stanton hated leaving the excitement of Boston. Trying to make the best of things, she threw herself into housekeeping, pickling, preserving, even making a game of getting her wash out on the line on Monday mornings before anybody else in town. All too soon, though, this kind of activity palled for her; her mind craved intellectual exercise.

Ever since her earliest childhood, she had been accustomed

to excel at schoolwork, and, after the death of her only brother when she was eleven, she had even tried to prove that her brain was as good as any boy's. "Oh, my daughter," her grieving father had moaned, "would that you were a boy!" And so Lizzie had pondered hard, decided the chief thing to do to equal a boy was to be courageous and learned, had taken up horseback riding to prove her courage, and had gone to the family pastor for secret lessons in Greek.

Progressing so fast that the pastor spoke with her father, she was sent to the academy on the hill, instead of just the common school, and soon she advanced right to the head of her class, winning a prize for her excellence in Greek. Then joyously telling herself that she had surely earned her father's approval, she raced to lay the prize on his desk. Evidently pleased, he kissed her on the forehead—but immediately sighed and said, "Ah, you should have been a boy!"

Despite his inability to accept Elizabeth as the equal of his departed son, Judge Cady had given her the best education open to a girl. He sent her to Mrs. Emma Willard's new Female Seminary in nearby Troy, New York; but the thought that higher education would unfit his daughter for comfortably enjoying normal female pursuits no doubt troubled him.

Now, increasingly restless in Seneca Falls, for once Elizabeth completely agreed with her father. Educating girls was wasteful, she sputtered to herself. Would she not be happier now if she had never even learned to read?

But her natural zest in living would not allow her to take such a dim view for long. Via books, papers, letters, she could still keep in touch with the world of ideas, even in sleepy Seneca Falls, and reading was one of her great pleasures. Among the highest moments she had to look forward to, now that Henry had given up the law and gone back to journalism, which kept him increasingly away from home, was the arrival of mail. For Lizzie Stanton herself, and for the future of all womankind, the arrival in Seneca Falls in the spring of 1848 of a long letter from Philadelphia was of portentous import.

The letter came from Lucretia Mott, now widely known as a remarkable figure on the national scene. Undaunted by mobs of ruffians, by murmurings even among her own Quaker brethren that she was overly forward, she had continued speaking out against slavery from every sort of platform. With her faithful James always by her side, she had traveled by coach through Virginia, gently taxing slaveowners themselves as unwitting tools of the forces of evil; in her simple slate-gray gown, she had stood before fashionable audiences in New York City to plead for support in her crusade.

To those who actually came out and heard her, even many of those who came prepared to jeer, Lucretia Mott more and more was taking on an almost saintly aura. Many newspaper editors, including some who scorned abolitionism as a terrible divisive force in American life, had already admitted Mrs. Mott to the company of noble Americans. Yet the prejudice of many men—and women—continued to thwart her wherever she went. No matter what their views on slavery were, the very notion of a woman daring to speak in public infuriated them. This constant abuse was enough to try the patience of any saint.

But it was not to complain about the status of woman that Mrs. Mott took up her pen and wrote to her dear young friend. Lizzie already had her own opinions on that subject, which she had often expressed in her letters to the older woman: "The more I think on the present condition of woman, the more I am impressed with the reality of her degradation," Lizzie had written. "The laws of our country, how unjust they are! Our customs, how vicious!"

The message that Mrs. Mott sat down to relay in the spring of 1848 was more personal. In her rather formal stilted prose, for she always found it so much easier to speak what was in her mind than write it, Mrs. Mott told Lizzie of the strain her own health had suffered in recent months. After continuous traveling and speaking, she felt so weak that her family was insisting that she rest. Within a matter of weeks, once her strength had been somewhat recouped, she was coming to visit her sister, in Auburn, New York, a short drive from Lizzie's own neighborhood.

Mrs. Mott's sister, Mrs. Martha Wright, had begged Lucretia to come spend the summer regaining her health and spirits in the fresh country air of Auburn, and since a Quaker conference was to be held in the area during the same period, it seemed to Lucretia more than a mere idle whim to pay the visit. Thus, she told Lizzie, there would surely be some opportunity to renew their old friendship in person during the next few months.

On a pleasant Friday morning in early July, Lizzie Stanton, having made every possible arrangement for the safekeeping of her boys during her absence, set out by pony cart to meet Mrs. Mott again. A tea party had been planned by one of sister Martha's friends, a Mrs. Richard Hunt, and it was there that Lucretia Mott and Elizabeth Cady Stanton greeted each other affectionately. "How goes it with thee?" Mrs. Mott asked; and then in a torrent of words, Lizzie proceeded to tell her.

By mail, and during a few precious visits in Boston, the two had continued to discuss their London resolve concerning the calling of a woman's rights convention. But one difficulty or another had always hampered their planning. Now with all of the pent-up force of recent personal discontent, particularly in regard to having no better mental occupation than col-

lecting pickle recipes, Lizzie Stanton insisted the time had
come to act.

No matter that they found themselves in a rural area, instead of a great city. Central New York was a veritable hotbed
for growing reform movements, said Mrs. Stanton, citing
various religious revivals and the active temperance agitation
in many nearby towns. As for downtrodden women, by her
own observation she felt certain there were farm wives and
daughters aplenty, disgusted over having to sew gloves every
night by candlelight to earn a few extra pennies, after having
already put in a full day at sweeping, cooking, milking, mend-
ing. They deserved the pennies for themselves, but the men
of the family took care of all money. Women like these would
surely come to their convention, Lizzie Stanton said triumphantly.

Still Mrs. Mott held back, wondering whether the height
of the haying season was not a bad time for holding any sort
of meeting locally. Now! said Lizzie Stanton. And she pre-
vailed. At Mrs. Hunt's tea table, as soon as the cloth had
been cleared, Lizzie grasped a pen and wrote a paragraph that
appeared on July 14, 1848, in the *Seneca County Courier:*

> WOMAN'S RIGHTS CONVENTION—A Convention to discuss
> the social, civil and religious condition and rights of
> women, will be held in the Wesleyan Chapel at Seneca
> Falls, N.Y., on Wednesday and Thursday, the 19th
> and 20th of July, current, commencing at 10 o'clock
> A.M. During the first day, the meeting will be exclu-
> sively for women, who are earnestly invited to attend.
> The public generally are invited to be present the sec-
> ond day, when Lucretia Mott of Philadelphia, and
> other ladies and gentlemen, will address the Conven-
> tion.

What could possibly be expected to follow the appearance

of this small notice in an obscure country newspaper? Elizabeth Cady Stanton expected the whole world to change—and she was right. Not nearly as swiftly as she hoped, nor perhaps quite as drastically, the whole world did change. Even in those areas where the name of Seneca Falls has never been heard, the echoes of words first spoken there more than a century ago are still sounding.

For no sooner had she sent off her one-paragraph announcement to the local weekly than Lizzie Stanton grasped her pen again. A program of some sort had to be planned for the convention, and speeches written. What was to be discussed? What action was to be taken? Only a few days remained before the convention would assemble, and it was imperative that something dramatic be accomplished.

Sitting around a sturdy mahogany center table in Mrs. Martha Wright's parlor on Sunday morning, just three days before the convention was to open, four other ladies listened as Lizzie Stanton thought aloud. Besides Mrs. Mott and Mrs. Wright, there were Mrs. Hunt and another sympathetic neighbor, Mrs. Mary Ann McClintock. Suppose, Lizzie Stanton suggested, suppose a document famous in American history were adopted as their model. Suppose the Declaration of Independence were taken, with its list of oppressions suffered by all Americans under the rule of King George, and suppose it were rewritten—to list the oppressions suffered by all women under the harsh rule of men.

"When, in the course of human events, . . ."* Mrs. Stanton's pen raced across the paper.

". . . We hold these truths to be self-evident: that all men *and women* are created equal . . ."

But then approving nods gave way to gasps of surprise. Carried beyond any past protest, inspired to state that there was one right forbidden to woman which was the basic right

* *Text of the Seneca Falls Declaration appears on pp. 183-186.*

of every citizen and from which all other rights logically flowed, Elizabeth Cady Stanton demanded . . . the right to vote. Even Lucretia Mott was aghast.

"Why, Lizzie," she said, "thee will make us ridiculous!" That was true. But Mrs. Stanton also made them famous. Although the ideas Lizzie Stanton expressed that day stunned everyone in the room, in time to come the sturdy mahogany table on which she wrote down the Seneca Falls Declaration would be taken to Washington, D.C., and placed on exhibit, along with the first airplanes and the first space capsules, in the Smithsonian Institution.

In 1848, it took courage to make such demands in public. And the public did come. Three days after she composed the Declaration, Mrs. Stanton read it in the Wesleyan Chapel to a larger audience than even she had expected. Farm women and town women—and a goodly sprinkling of men, who on the whole seemed sympathetic—crowded the chapel benches. Altogether about three hundred persons had appeared.

Although the plan had been to limit attendance on the first day to females only, the men who arrived were not refused admission. Among the male contingent, one expected observer was, however, missing. On returning home after a trip, Henry B. Stanton had been just in time to hear his wife rehearse reading her paper, and he had been severely shaken. He would have nothing to do with such a business, he fumed. If she insisted on standing up in public to read what she had written, he would not suffer to listen, he would leave town instead. Mrs. Stanton said she would read it; Mr. Stanton did leave, for a few days.

Thus he was not a witness when his wife rose in the crowded hall and started:

"I should feel exceedingly diffident to appear before you at this time, having never before spoken in public, were I not nerved by a sense of right and duty, did I not feel that the time had come for the question of woman's wrongs to be laid before the public, did I not believe that woman herself must do this work; for woman alone can understand the height, the depth, the length and breadth of her degradation. . . ."

Then Mrs. Stanton read her Declaration.

No thunder or lightning marked the moment, but for two days there was much earnest discussion in the country meeting hall. At the close of the second day, sixty-eight women and thirty-two men walked forward one by one, to sign their names to the historic Declaration of Sentiments.

In addition, the entire assemblage adopted eleven resolutions. Over ten of these, no controversy arose; these were resolutions demanding equal rights for women in varying phases of daily life—in colleges and universities, in trades and professions, in courts of law and in codes of law. The eleventh resolution, demanding for women equal rights with men in the nation's polling booths, also was adopted, but by a lesser margin; for Lucretia Mott had known whereof she spoke when she had warned that so radical a new idea would cast ridicule on the whole program.

But neither Mrs. Mott—nor Henry Stanton—had foreseen the full extent of the reaction that would be provoked. Within the next several weeks, as word of the Seneca Falls goings-on reached them, newspaper editors in many places sharpened their quills. The Albany, New York, *Mechanic's Advocate* carried the headline: WOMEN OUT OF THEIR LATITUDE.

Other editors wrote sarcastically of the female "insurrection," and wondered if "the reign of petticoats" was dawning. More commonly, though, they treated the whole affair as a grand joke bound to amuse sensible citizens. Said the Lowell, Massachusetts, *Courier:*

PROGRESS—The women folks have just held a Convention up in N.Y. State, and passed a sort of "bill of rights," affirming it their right to vote, to be teachers, legislators, lawyers, divines, and do all the sundries the "lords" may, and of right do now. They should have resolved at the same time that it was obligatory also upon the "lords" aforesaid, to wash dishes, scour up, handle the broom, darn stockings, patch breeches, scold the servants, dress in the latest fashion, wear trinkets, look beautiful, and be as fascinating as these blessed morsels of humanity whom God gave to preserve that rough animal man, in something like reasonable civilization. Progress! Progress forever!

Enter
Susan

4

Having taken the first step, what next?

The Seneca Falls Declaration had said: ". . . We shall use every instrumentality within our power to effect our object. We shall employ agents, circulate tracts, petition the State and National legislatures. . . ."

But the most important "instrumentality" in the great campaign ahead had yet to be enlisted. She was a tall, self-possessed schoolmarm, twenty-eight years old in 1848. Reading newspaper quips about "The Hen Convention," Susan Brownell Anthony laughed heartily.

Miss Anthony was principal of the girls' department of a private academy in Canajoharie, New York, not too distant from Seneca Falls; but even had she felt the impulse to be present at the historic meeting there, she had no way of knowing about it in advance because the *Seneca County Courier* did not circulate in her area. Once informed of what had already occurred, her reaction was purely amused.

Then on a subsequent weekend, she went home to visit her earnest Quaker parents on their farm near Rochester, and found them so fired up about the woman question that she

began to take it more seriously. Only two weeks after the
Seneca Falls meeting, a similar and larger gathering had been
held in Rochester; and being more than willing to lend their
support to any worthy reform, the Anthony family had turned
out to hear what Mrs. Mott and Mrs. Stanton had to say.
Mr. and Mrs. Anthony and another of their daughters had all
signed their names to the resolutions adopted, even the resolution demanding for women the right to vote.

That surprised Susan Anthony. Her father was a strict
Quaker of the old school, a complete pacifist who held it
wrong to play an active part in any government which considered war a possible course of action. He himself had never
voted. Yet now he chose to endorse the principle of votes for
women.

From being amused, and teasingly telling her father she
would like to meet these women who had changed his mind,
Susan proceeded to think over the whole woman's rights
question as she weeded and pruned her favorite berry patch.
By now, she was tired of teaching; but, no matter that she was
still trim and handsome enough to marry if she chose to,
she could not imagine spending her life waiting on any man.
What she craved was a worth-while cause to which she could
devote every ounce of her energy. Woman's rights? As a young
woman of exceptional drive, she had already come against
various barriers holding back her sex when she was going to
school herself and later when she was searching for work. But
another cause interested her more—the cause of temperance.

Returning to Canajoharie, Miss Anthony plunged with re-
newed zeal into working after school hours for the local chap-
ter of a society calling itself the Daughters of Temperance.
This was the female auxiliary of the Sons of Temperance, an
association composed largely of clergymen who wanted every
man to sign a pledge never to touch liquor. Being a born

reformer, Susan was satisfied—for a time.

But all reformers are rebels, because they aim to change society. Both in this sense and in the generally accepted sense of being prone to resist authority, Susan Anthony was a born rebel, too hot a rebel for the comparatively tame cause that temperance was then. The example set by her family was irresistible.

Not that her parents were flaming firebrands, but they did have an unusually powerful drive to do what they thought was right, regardless of other people's opinions. Their marriage itself was evidence of this. Years earlier, Daniel Anthony had defied Quaker tradition by courting a girl who was not a Quaker, who delighted in singing and dancing and wearing bright ribbons in her hair; then for his sake, she had turned sober as any Quaker elder could wish. But Susan had often heard the story of how her mother had defiantly danced at a party till the cocks crowed just a few days before the wedding, in one last frivolous fling. This had happened in western Massachusetts, where Susan was born on February 15, 1820. Her birthplace was Adams, a prosperous little trading center in the picturesque Berkshire hill country. Her father operated a small cotton mill there.

When Susan was six, the family moved to New York State, and their new neighbors found them upright, hard-working people, but decidedly independent in their ways. Daniel Anthony refused to modify his own ideas about religious questions, even when the majority of the local Quaker community disagreed with him. As for his wife, a fondness for music and finery still lurked within Mrs. Anthony, and also a deep sort of discontent. Although she bore eight children—Susan was the second—she never would permit anybody to speak of an impending addition to the family, and she obviously dreaded each such event almost unbearably. Her second daughter marked this well.

An extremely intelligent child, Susan could read even before she began to go to school. And she remembered demanding to be taught long division not many months later, despite the fact that the subject was considered too difficult for much bigger girls; besides, only boys were supposed to have the need for any such advanced mathematical skill. But Susan had noticed boys working at problems that looked interesting, and refused to be left out. That was her first rebellion.

When she finished her schooling and became a teacher, she showed her rebel streak more openly. Then Canajoharie, which had expected a prim Quaker of a schoolmarm, instead found itself welcoming an amazingly stylish young lady. For Miss Susan Anthony, as soon as she had earned the money to make it possible, calmly reversed her mother's example. She put aside Quaker gray, and bought quite an elegant wardrobe.

She was methodical enough to note down in her diary exactly what she spent: $5.50 for a white silk-ribbed bonnet, $8.00 for a fox muff, $22.50 for an embroidered shawl. She also purchased sufficient plum-covered silk, at $2.00 a yard, to have made for her a gown taken from a model in *Godey's Lady's Book,* complete with ruffled skirt draped over a hoop, and a cape edged with fringes; exclusive of trimmings, the dress took fully eighteen yards of material.

Adorned thus, Miss Anthony next took up dancing. Nor could she help attracting partners, being such a fine figure of a young woman, with the glossiest dark brown hair. Yet something in her nature would not let her kick up her heels for long. Rebellion against her stern upbringing had no doubt been inevitable, considering the independence of her character. But very soon she discovered that she had no real taste for dancing or flirting.

Precisely what put her back on a more sober track she

Susan B. Anthony.

never discussed. One suspects that a drunken man had something to do with it. At a ball she attended in her new plum-colored finery, there occurred an unfortunate experience which she described only guardedly in her diary.

"My fancy for attending dances is fully satisfied," she wrote. "I certainly shall not attend another unless I can have a total abstinence man to accompany me, and not one whose highest delight is to make a fool of himself."

From then on, even men who never drank a drop of wine appeared to interest her less than the cause of temperance did. In Canajoharie, various high-minded ladies had formed the Daughters of Temperance, and Miss Anthony had already joined them before her visit to her family in Rochester. After spending some weeks in the reform atmosphere of her own home, when she returned to Canajoharie for the fall term she seemed wholly committed to the cause. But her rebel streak was too strong; it craved bolder work. Soon her passionate enlistment in the war against alcohol led her to the great partnership of her life—with Elizabeth Cady Stanton.

So intertwined were the various reform campaigns agitating America in the middle of the nineteenth century that an anti-slavery rally was the occasion for the first meeting of the schoolmarm temperance organizer and the matron founder of the woman suffrage movement. That meeting took place early in 1851, on a street corner in Seneca Falls.

William Lloyd Garrison himself had come to lecture in Seneca Falls, and both ladies came to see and hear the famous abolition leader. By now, Mrs. Stanton was enormously engrossed in her woman's rights work, speaking, writing, circulating petitions; still she was not too engrossed to take time for such an important local event as a Garrison lecture. Indeed she made sure to engage the speaker to come dine at her home after the conclusion of his meeting.

Walking home with Mr. Garrison, in quite some haste because of her uncertainty over what her boys had been up to in her absence, Mrs. Stanton was stopped by an acquaintance in the street—Mrs. Amelia Bloomer, the local assistant postmistress. In a few years, Mrs. Bloomer's name was to become famous; it was already known beyond the neighborhood served by her post office. Mrs. Bloomer published, as a small extra income source, a little newspaper she called *The Lily,* in token of her determination to promote purity within its pages. *The Lily* took a strong temperance stand. Mrs. Bloomer had been sought out by one of her readers, a visitor to Seneca Falls who wished a favor. Remembering her own quip about wanting to meet the woman who could change her father's mind, Miss Susan B. Anthony had found some one who could introduce her to Mrs. Stanton.

Ever after, Mrs. Stanton would recall her first glimpse of Susan's good earnest face and genial smile, waiting to greet her. Dressed in gray again, but with pale blue ribbons on her hat, Miss Anthony looked the perfection of neatness and sobriety. Thought Mrs. Stanton to herself, I really must invite this nice young woman home to dinner with us. But after chatting comfortably for a few moments, the mother suddenly recollected her youngsters and grasped Mr. Garrison's arm; quite forgetting her hospitable impulse toward Miss Anthony, she hurried the visiting gentleman along, leaving the visiting lady to find a meal for herself elsewhere.

Both ladies laughed about this later. For within two years, "Aunt Susan" was a favorite with the Stanton boys, and one of the most extraordinary teams in American history had started on its long and fruitful association.

In keeping with the pattern that had already been set, it was frustration over being treated shabbily by the Sons of Temperance that converted Susan B. Anthony to the feminist cause. Like Lucretia Mott with her half a pair of scissors, Miss Anthony discovered that a separate woman's group could accomplish little, and she set about trying to unite the sons and daughters in one general temperance society. Meeting some slight success at first, she managed to become selected as a delegate to a state-wide convention of the New York Sons of Temperance, in Albany in 1852.

In this case, the lady delegates were assigned seats right in the meeting hall. But no sooner had Miss Anthony risen to speak on a motion before the assembly than she was silenced by the chairman. The female delegates had been admitted, he said blandly, not to speak, but merely to *listen and learn*. Blazing with anger, Miss Anthony walked out of the meeting, and a few other ladies left with her.

Why are you surprised? Mrs. Stanton asked, when in the normal course of reform activity the two women crossed each other's paths again. Why do you not recognize that woman's rights must come first? Miss Anthony was not ready to be convinced. Aroused by a splendid sense of purpose now, she quit her teaching to give full time to temperance. If the men looked down on her, she would show them: she would organize the biggest and most effective temperance society New York State had ever seen, and hold the biggest temperance convention ever held, and then the men would change their tune.

By writing hundreds of letters, publicizing her plans, begging money to pay necessary expenses, hiring halls for countless small preliminary meetings, by working tirelessly for months, Miss Anthony accomplished the first part of her program. Her Woman's State Temperance Convention in Rochester was a rousing success. Even Mrs. Stanton let herself be deflected from her own main objective to appear as a speaker, and then she allowed her name to be put forward as the new group's president. Miss Anthony and Mrs. Bloomer were jointly chosen as its secretaries.

With a membership of more than one thousand, with an active petition drive underway, Miss Anthony and Mrs. Bloomer were not surprised to be invited to the next temperance men's convention. So the plan had worked! But on arriving in Syracuse for this meeting, the two ladies were met by an embarrassed minister. There had been an error, he told them. They had best retire.

No, she would not, said Miss Anthony. Somewhat less militantly, Mrs. Bloomer followed her into the meeting, where their appearance provoked a storm. Although much of the membership of the men's group consisted of conservative clergymen, the gentlemen hooted and shouted while Miss Anthony tried to make herself heard.

Women were entitled to be represented, she wanted to explain. But the audience would not listen. Women had no business bursting into meetings this way, irate ministers boomed. Next thing, the whole world would be turned upside down. To the overwhelming approval of the assemblage, Miss Anthony and her companion were led out of the hall.

Then Susan Anthony could doubt no longer. Mrs. Stanton was correct: freedom for woman had to come before any other cause. With the organizing genius she had already begun to demonstrate, the former schoolmarm now plunged into the great work that would ever after be associated with her name.

Early in the 1850's, when Miss Anthony began her half century of battling for woman's rights, the struggle was still so new that no coherent program had yet been formulated. There was instead a series of flurries on several fronts.

Back in 1848, the year when Mrs. Mott and Mrs. Stanton had taken their first open action, a significant legal victory for womankind had also been won. In that year, the legislature of New York had enacted a measure substantially liberalizing married women's property rights. Under the revision, which other states also were considering and soon would adopt, husbands no longer had complete control of all property inherited by their wives. Although the change did not go far enough to satisfy many of the reform-minded, it nevertheless marked a definite departure from the old common law system holding that married women had absolutely no property rights.

Ironically, reformers could claim less credit in this case than the forces of conservatism could. For the main thrust in pushing legislatures to amend the old law came from wealthy families unwilling to see their daughters' fortunes threatened by profligate sons-in-law. However, there had indeed been petitions on the subject from other, more radical elements as well; there were bound to be, in these amazing times.

For amazing they certainly were. Over in Europe, a tidal wave of revolutionary uprisings had just toppled half a dozen established governments. In the New World, the Mexican War had just ended . . . California was part of the United States . . . GOLD had been discovered in California. And steam was changing every facet of life, with steam-driven locomotives conquering distance, steam-powered factories producing beyond the wildest dreams, steam printing presses spewing out thousands of newspapers every hour, spreading the latest word flashed over new telegraph lines.

Inevitably these were times of great social upheaval. Women by the thousand were leaving farm kitchens and city slum kitchens to work in factories. Whether anybody wished this to happen or not, the process could not be stopped; the forces industrializing America were too strong.

Thus the times were ripe for an assault on the old laws

and customs limiting woman's rights. In New York, Miss Elizabeth Blackwell soberly presented herself to study medicine at a small upstate college, and became the nation's first woman doctor; Miss Antoinette Brown, refusing to be daunted, was ordained as the nation's first female minister; in Ohio, girls were admitted to Oberlin College on the same basis as male students; in Massachusetts, Mount Holyoke Seminary founded by Mary Lyon was offering a college education to the daughters of New England; and in Massachusetts, the musical-voiced Miss Lucy Stone was lecturing up and down the state on a woman's rights crusade of her own.

It was in this electric climate of change that Susan Anthony entered on her life's work.

Of
Bloomers
and
Ballots

5

Hi! Ho! In rain and snow,
The bloomer now is all the go!
Twenty tailors take the stitches,
Plenty o' women wear the britches!

Sung out from behind fences, shouted down from city doorsteps, this jolly chant greeted Miss Anthony wherever she went. Groups of chortling boys, even grown men, called after her morning, noon, and night. There was no doubt about it, the woman's rights movement was on every tongue. Still Miss Anthony could not but wonder a bit grimly whether the public interest might possibly have been aroused in some less painful manner.

Had she searched her mind for some sure method of attracting attention to her cause, she could not have thought up a more effective device than the bloomer. Yet, like so many other inspirations, it was an accidental discovery. And although it certainly served a very real purpose, it also caused many good women untold anguish.

The story of the bloomer started when a cousin of Mrs. Stanton's paid her a visit in Seneca Falls. An unusually graceful woman, with a romantic streak that led her to admire Lord Byron enormously, Mrs. Elizabeth Smith Miller appeared wearing a bizarre costume she had designed herself, based on what she imagined one of Byron's Turkish heroines would wear. This was a loose but belted knee-length tunic, worn over a pair of long, floppy trousers. On Mrs. Miller, even this strange outfit looked attractive.

Lizzie Stanton was enchanted. It was altogether a most becoming costume, she said enthusiastically, and exceedingly convenient for walking in all kinds of weather. At least on the second count, she was right.

In the early 1850's, fashion sternly decreed that all ladies must wear trailing skirts held out like a bell by five or six starched petticoats, and this whole assembly was a terrible mud-catcher. Furthermore, the wearer of any such attire had to be additionally hampered by a tight, boned corset to hold in her waist, and often a framework of hoops to expand her nether regions. Taking even a short stroll under such circumstances was not easy; climbing stairs with a lamp in one hand, a baby in the other, presented almost insupportable difficulties, particularly when it had to be remembered that a lady must never let the public even suspect that she possessed legs.

"What incredible freedom!" Mrs. Stanton exclaimed to Mrs. Miller. And immediately she made herself a copy of Mrs. Miller's costume.

Being short and quite plump by now, Mrs. Stanton presented something less than a graceful picture in her new garb. But she cheerfully persevered in wearing it around the house because she had another new baby, and the convenience of the trousers when it came to stair-climbing positively delighted her. Then, since she had become such a practiced reformer, she could not but conclude that all women would be

Elizabeth Cady Stanton in her bloomer costume.

better off if they wore the new costume; suddenly, dress reform became her main passion.

So she induced her dear Susan to copy her pattern; she mailed sewing instructions to all her acquaintances, and soon a few dozen dedicated feminists were hesitantly appearing in public in trousers. But some faster way to spread the dress reform had to be found, Mrs. Stanton decided. Then a spendid idea occurred to her, and she took a set of drawings to the publisher of *The Lily*. Mrs. Bloomer obligingly printed them, in utter innocence of what would happen as a result. Within a few months, *bloomers* were all the rage!

Despite the uproarious reaction on the part of almost all men and, it must be admitted, most women, Mrs. Stanton would not admit defeat for more than two years. In that period, she and several hundred other ladies dared the hilarity of the multitude by walking out in their pantaloons. Lucy Stone wore them and so did the Grimké sisters, although the dignified Mrs. Mott did not. At a ball in Akron, Ohio, more than sixty young ladies appeared in the bloomer costume.

One plain-spoken friend of Mrs. Stanton's wrote in a letter to a mutual acquaintance: "Imagine her then in a full black satin frock cut off at the knee, with Turkish trowsers of the same material, her wrap a double shawl and on her head a great hideous bonnet. I have seen scarecrows that did credit to farmers' boys' ingenuity, but never one better calculated to scare all birds, beasts and human beings." Even Mrs. Stanton's oldest son, by now away at boarding school, begged his mother not to embarrass him by visiting him in her trousers. So at last, in 1854, Mrs. Stanton relented—and lengthened all her skirts.

The surrender came not a moment too soon for Susan Anthony. Only a day before receiving word to let down her skirt hems, she had written in a letter: ". . . have been in the streets and the printing offices all day long, had rude and vulgar men stare me out of countenance and heard them say as I opened a door, 'There comes my bloomer!' Oh, hated name! Oh, I cannot, cannot bear it any longer!"

Relieved that she no longer had to bear such abuse, Miss Anthony felt a new freedom to concentrate on the serious work in which she was engaged. By virtue of the bloomer furor, the woman's rights movement had become a common topic of conversation; now she hoped to be able to make it a truly effective political force.

Beyond question, Mrs. Stanton was the thinker of the movement, plotting its basic course brilliantly, even though from time to time she simply could not resist a zigzag when bloomers, or some other diversion, distracted her. But equally beyond question, it was Susan Anthony who took on the responsibility for doing all the many hard and thankless jobs that had to be done if success was ever to be achieved. Even Henry Stanton joked over their wonderfully effective division of labor. "You stir up Susan," he told his wife, "and she stirs up the world."

In the winter of 1854, in Mrs. Stanton's judgment the time had come for women to make their first major effort to win the right to vote. She chose New York State as their test battleground. And then it was Miss Anthony who had to find a way to put the issue before the public.

The extraordinary talent for organizing that she had already showed in her temperance campaign provided her with a plan. It was a remarkable plan for the 1850's, when nothing like it had yet been attempted. What Miss Anthony did was to divide the entire state into sixty districts, and then appoint a "captain" for each district. Her own task, by far the hardest, would be to supervise the entire operation.

Up until now, the only real weapon that had been

thought of by her fellow feminists was the weapon of words. By holding meetings, making speeches, passing resolutions, they aimed to attract attention to their grievances, hammering away with words and more words until they converted multitudes of people. Then it seemed logical that lawmakers would be moved to act. This kind of propaganda drive was enormously important and could not be neglected, Miss Anthony was sure, but she had the sort of direct mind that was impatient with mere words. She wanted to bring women's demands straight to the legislators, to present the lawmakers with overwhelming proof that thousands of women were tired of waiting and wanted reform, at once. Her weapon was the petition.

Petitions had been tried before, but only to a limited extent. In the recent past, reformers of every stripe had been collecting signatures on statements asking some change in the law, and such documents were constantly being presented to lawmaking bodies. But thus far, petitions on issues of interest to feminists had been individual efforts, or at most representative of just a small group. It remained for Susan Anthony to see that proper organizing was essential, to secure a massive weight of signatures.

So while Mrs. Stanton, surrounded by children, was busy washing dishes, sewing, baking, thinking, her dear Susan spent the worst of a New York winter battling snowdrifts and apathy. Pushing on from town to town, in any conveyance that she could find to cope with the snow-covered roads, she tirelessly tacked up announcements of meetings, hired halls, coached speakers, spoke herself, forced herself to beg money to pay necessary expenses. Like a traveling peddler, she even went from door to door carrying petitions.

This was the most agonizing task of all. Door after door was slammed in her face. "We have husbands to look after

our rights!" she was told time after time. "You're a trouble-
maker. Go away!" Such blind refusal to face facts, even on
the part of careworn farm women whose husbands treated
them like some dumb animals, infuriated Miss Anthony almost beyond bearing. But often enough to keep her from
utter despair, she met quite a different reaction. "Bless you!"
the wife of a local banker would murmur. "I wish I had the
courage to do what you are doing."

By the end of almost every day, her toes were frostbitten,
her back ached so that she could hardly stand. Some mornings, awakening in an icy room of a miserable inn where
even the breakfast would be indigestible, she wondered how
she could go on for another day, but she always did. By
spring, Miss Anthony had covered fifty-four of New York's
sixty counties.

Then it was back to Rochester, for a well-earned rest with
her family. Yet even there her days were filled; Mrs. Stanton
needed the leisure to write some speeches, and so her young
had been deposited with the Anthonys for a farm vacation.

Acting on her acute political sense, Miss Anthony had decided to combine the petition-presenting with a state-wide
woman's rights convention. She reasoned that the legislators
would be more strongly convinced that the women of the
state were becoming aroused if a substantial number of
women were convening under their very noses.

Thus there were numerous addresses and resolutions that
had to be written in advance, and it was in this area that Mrs.
Stanton shone. "Whenever I take my pen in hand, I seem to
be mounted on stilts," Miss Anthony complained. Mrs. Stanton had no such problem; she was a swift, effective writer.
Nevertheless, she was taking special pains with one of the
papers she was preparing.

The legislature of New York had graciously agreed to hear

a representative of the women, and had appointed a committee to consider what they had to say. Presented with this unprecedented opportunity, Mrs. Stanton wanted to make the best possible impression. Thus she took a special journey, daring her father's disapproval in order to use his law library for her research.

She was determined to have solid facts to back up her demands. Besides the ballot, she was also going to seek correction of several long-standing legal disabilities afflicting women; in particular, she would stress the need for new laws giving married women control of any money they earned, and giving them the guardianship of their children in cases of divorce. To bolster her argument about the imperative necessity for reform, she desired as many instances as possible of the unjust laws currently in effect.

Mrs. Stanton's father could not be ignorant of what she was up to, for newspapers had already carried mention of the impending hearing. Old Judge Cady did not appear to have mellowed appreciably. His greeting to his daughter was the question: What had been lacking in her own life that could make her so bitter about the wrongs done to her sex? Had she herself been made to suffer? No, she assured him, but in the very office where they were speaking she had listened many times during her childhood while other women wept at being told the law could not help them. Hesitantly she read to her father what she had written, and waited for his opinion.

"Well . . . well," he said at last, and there was a strange expression on his face that, had she been his son, would surely have been pride. "You have made your points clear and strong," he finally admitted. "But . . . I think I can find you even more cruel laws than those you have quoted." And so after decades of shaking his head mournfully at her unwomanly behavior, he spent the next hour helping her go through his lawbooks.

But if Judge Cady was impressed, New York's distinguished lawmakers reacted quite otherwise. After Mrs. Stanton finished speaking to them, the special committee appointed to consider her address and Miss Anthony's petitions deliberated privately before producing a report. This was read aloud while the ladies in the visitors' gallery sat, almost unable to believe what they heard. However, the report was reprinted in many newspapers, so there could be no doubt about the wording. It said:

> The Committee is composed of married and single men. The bachelors on the Committee, with becoming diffidence, have left the subject pretty much to the married gentlemen. They have considered it with the aid of the light they have before them and the experience married life has given them. Thus aided, they are enabled to state that the ladies always have the best place and choicest tidbit at the table. They always have the best seat in the cars, carriages and sleighs; the warmest place in the winter and the coolest place in the summer. A lady's dress costs three times as much as that of a gentleman; and, at the present time, with the prevailing fashion, one lady occupies three times as much space in the world as a gentleman.
>
> It has thus appeared to the married gentlemen of your Committee, being a majority (the bachelors being silent for the reason mentioned and also probably for the further reason that they are still suitors for the favors of the gentler sex), that if there is any inequity or oppression in the case, the gentlemen are the sufferers. They, however, have presented no petitions for redress, having, doubtless, made up their minds to yield to an inevitable destiny.
>
> On the whole, the Committee have concluded to recommend no measure, except as they have observed several instances in which husband and wife have signed the same petition. In such case, they would

recommend the parties to apply for a law authorizing them to change dress, that the husband may wear petticoats and the wife the breeches, and thus indicate to their neighbors and the public the true relation in which they stand to each other.

That was the response to American women's first formal request for the right to vote.

Listening to the roars of laughter sweeping the chamber, Susan Anthony coldly took stock. Next time, she told herself, next time she would get more names, and still more names on her petitions. Four thousand names she had gotten this past winter, by dint of much backbreaking effort, but four thousand names had not been enough.

Perhaps if all of the four thousand had been *voters,* then even four thousand would have been heard more respectfully. Any elected body would have to be more courteous to such a number of voters. But most of her names were women's names, and *women could not vote.* There was the heart of the problem!

Without the right to vote, how could women impress the seriousness of their wrongs on any elected officials? It was so easy to ignore the women, or merely to ridicule them, as in the present case. But many of these men had wives who might influence them. If sufficient numbers of women could be aroused to demand their rights, then change must come. And dauntlessly Miss Anthony determined to go forth once more, in quest of many times four thousand signatures.

"It's the Negro's Hour!"

6

Meanwhile in Maine, the meek little wife of a professor of religion had, quite unbeknownst to Miss Anthony, been writing a book that would make a big difference to her own planning. Mrs. Harriet Beecher Stowe's *Uncle Tom's Cabin* had an enormous impact on the whole course of American history; and among its many side effects, it set back the schedule of the woman's rights campaign for at least a generation.

President Lincoln himself was said to have smiled wryly when he was introduced to Mrs. Stowe, and then remarked: "So here is the little lady who started this big war." Though Mr. Lincoln was exaggerating somewhat the book's role in precipitating the Civil War, he did have reason to acknowledge it as a factor in the nation's willingness to go to battle. By painting the evil of slavery in such stark, emotional strokes that no reader could fail to be moved, Mrs. Stowe made abolitionism respectable.

During the middle of the 1850's, when her book was selling by the tens of thousands, countless good people who had tended to push aside the unpleasant question of what was to be done about the Negro slaves in the South suddenly began flocking to anti-slavery meetings. At the same time, in the South itself a flaming rage grew over what it considered unjustified meddling. Throughout the country, there was very little energy left over for other causes, such as the woman's rights movement.

But in the North, woman's rights had already progressed too far to stop completely. For two reasons, hardly any interest had been stirred in the South: on the one hand, the traditional Southern culture, based upon chivalrous days of old, allowed no opportunities for ladies to step off their pedestals and attend meetings; and on the other, the almost universal hatred in which abolitionists were held below the Mason-Dixon line easily rubbed off to tar any reformers even vaguely associated with anti-slavery agitation. However, dozens of exceptional women were leading the feminist battle in almost every Northern and Western state.

Even during the hectic months when the slavery issue was on every tongue and the horror of open war moved ever closer, Frances Dana Gage of Ohio—the "Aunt Fanny" who wrote popular stories for children—kept organizing women's conventions. So did Clarinda Howard Nichols of Vermont, who edited an influential New England newspaper and even carried the banner of woman's rights into the Western territories when she visited her pioneer sons. And there were still the lecturers, Abby Kelley, now Abby Kelley Foster, and Lucy Stone, now known as Mrs. Stone because she and her husband had agreed she did not have to lose her own name simply because she was married. Both these ladies continued to draw large audiences.

There were also several Negro women emerging as outstanding speakers for the cause. By far the most famous of these was a former slave who, on gaining her freedom, took the name Sojourner Truth and began traveling the back roads of America, standing up in churches and wherever she could find an audience, to plead for freedom for her people. A giantess of a woman, with a voice that vibrated to the furthest reaches of any assemblage, she developed a spellbinding power that became almost legendary. From preaching freedom for Negroes, she came to preach freedom for women, no matter what the color of their skin.

It was at a woman's rights convention in Akron, Ohio, when hecklers began drowning out a gentle-voiced speaker, that Sojourner Truth was first moved to enlist her strong voice in the cause of freedom for women. Rising from the corner where she had been sitting, she moved solemnly forward, laid her old bonnet on the floor, and then spoke with a fervor those who heard her would never forget.

"The man over there says women need to be helped into carriages and lifted over ditches, and to have the best place everywhere," she started. "Nobody ever helps me into carriages or over puddles, or gives me the best place—and ain't I a woman? Look at my arm! I have ploughed and planted and gathered into barns and no man could head me—and ain't I a woman? I could work as much and eat as much as a man—when I could get it—and bear the lash as well! And ain't I a woman? I have borne thirteen children, and seen most of 'em sold into slavery, and when I cried out with my mother's grief, none but Jesus heard me—and ain't I a woman?"

In cities and in small towns, women like these continued to demand emancipation for their sex. Right up until the firing on Fort Sumter, regional conventions were held every year, despite the increasing difficulty of organizing any effort of this sort in such troubled times. Foremost among the organizers was still Miss Susan B. Anthony.

"Whenever I saw that stately Quaker girl coming across my

Yᵉ MAY SESSION OF Yᵉ WOMAN'S RIGHTS CONVENTION—Yᵉ ORATOR OF Yᵉ DAY DENOUNCING Yᵉ LORDS OF CREATION.

A cartoonist's view of a woman's rights convention.

Library of Congress

"It's the Negro's Hour!"

6

Meanwhile in Maine, the meek little wife of a professor of religion had, quite unbeknownst to Miss Anthony, been writing a book that would make a big difference to her own planning. Mrs. Harriet Beecher Stowe's *Uncle Tom's Cabin* had an enormous impact on the whole course of American history; and among its many side effects, it set back the schedule of the woman's rights campaign for at least a generation.

President Lincoln himself was said to have smiled wryly when he was introduced to Mrs. Stowe, and then remarked: "So here is the little lady who started this big war." Though Mr. Lincoln was exaggerating somewhat the book's role in precipitating the Civil War, he did have reason to acknowledge it as a factor in the nation's willingness to go to battle. By painting the evil of slavery in such stark, emotional strokes that no reader could fail to be moved, Mrs. Stowe made abolitionism respectable.

During the middle of the 1850's, when her book was selling by the tens of thousands, countless good people who had tended to push aside the unpleasant question of what was to be done about the Negro slaves in the South suddenly began flocking to anti-slavery meetings. At the same time, in the South itself a flaming rage grew over what it considered unjustified meddling. Throughout the country, there was very little energy left over for other causes, such as the woman's rights movement.

But in the North, woman's rights had already progressed too far to stop completely. For two reasons, hardly any interest had been stirred in the South: on the one hand, the traditional Southern culture, based upon chivalrous days of old, allowed no opportunities for ladies to step off their pedestals and attend meetings; and on the other, the almost universal hatred in which abolitionists were held below the Mason-Dixon line easily rubbed off to tar any reformers even vaguely associated with anti-slavery agitation. However, dozens of exceptional women were leading the feminist battle in almost every Northern and Western state.

Even during the hectic months when the slavery issue was on every tongue and the horror of open war moved ever closer, Frances Dana Gage of Ohio—the "Aunt Fanny" who wrote popular stories for children—kept organizing women's conventions. So did Clarinda Howard Nichols of Vermont, who edited an influential New England newspaper and even carried the banner of woman's rights into the Western territories when she visited her pioneer sons. And there were still the lecturers, Abby Kelley, now Abby Kelley Foster, and Lucy Stone, now known as Mrs. Stone because she and her husband had agreed she did not have to lose her own name simply because she was married. Both these ladies continued to draw large audiences.

There were also several Negro women emerging as outstanding speakers for the cause. By far the most famous of these was a former slave who, on gaining her freedom, took

the name Sojourner Truth and began traveling the back roads of America, standing up in churches and wherever she could find an audience, to plead for freedom for her people. A giantess of a woman, with a voice that vibrated to the furthest reaches of any assemblage, she developed a spellbinding power that became almost legendary. From preaching freedom for Negroes, she came to preach freedom for women, no matter what the color of their skin.

It was at a woman's rights convention in Akron, Ohio, when hecklers began drowning out a gentle-voiced speaker, that Sojourner Truth was first moved to enlist her strong voice in the cause of freedom for women. Rising from the corner where she had been sitting, she moved solemnly forward, laid her old bonnet on the floor, and then spoke with a fervor those who heard her would never forget.

"The man over there says women need to be helped into carriages and lifted over ditches, and to have the best place everywhere," she started. "Nobody ever helps me into carriages or over puddles, or gives me the best place—and ain't I a woman? Look at my arm! I have ploughed and planted and gathered into barns and no man could head me—and ain't I a woman? I could work as much and eat as much as a man—when I could get it—and bear the lash as well! And ain't I a woman? I have borne thirteen children, and seen most of 'em sold into slavery, and when I cried out with my mother's grief, none but Jesus heard me—and ain't I a woman?"

In cities and in small towns, women like these continued to demand emancipation for their sex. Right up until the firing on Fort Sumter, regional conventions were held every year, despite the increasing difficulty of organizing any effort of this sort in such troubled times. Foremost among the organizers was still Miss Susan B. Anthony.

"Whenever I saw that stately Quaker girl coming across my

lawn," Mrs. Stanton wrote later, "I knew that some happy convocation of the sons of Adam was to be set by the ears, by one of our appeals or resolutions." For Susan's little traveling case, on being opened, always proved stuffed with facts, such as statistics about women robbed of their property, shut out of some college, half paid for some work—"injustice enough," Mrs. Stanton added, "to turn any woman's thoughts from stockings and puddings."

So then these two gifted collaborators would get out their pens and begin composing speeches again. While the Stanton children, now totaling seven, would watch with varying degrees of patience, their mother and their Aunt Susan would spread papers all over the dining room table. Within the next few weeks, the words written there would ring out from some distant platform.

Even in these troubled times, some progress on the woman's rights front was achieved. In 1860, Mrs. Stanton once more appeared in Albany, this time speaking before a joint session of both houses of the legislature. Her six years of speeches, Susan's travels, and the labors of the other women had not been in vain. This time the lawmakers' reaction was more civil; within a few months they passed a bill giving married women control of their own wages, and also the right to start lawsuits in their own names instead of having to be represented by their husbands.

But then the first cannon boomed at Fort Sumter in South Carolina. From Washington, President Lincoln telegraphed every governor, asking for troops to save the Union. While eleven states of the South defiantly formed the Confederate States of America, in Massachusetts and New York, in Ohio and Pennsylvania, regiments of volunteers marched aboard southbound trains, singing: "We are coming, Father Abraham . . ." Mrs. Stanton and Miss Anthony fully realized that they must hold off on their own campaign—for the ballot—until the larger issues of the Civil War were settled.

Being so accustomed to activity, they could not rest, however. They added their strength to the swelling movement led by their old abolitionist friends, aimed now at forcing President Lincoln to emancipate all slaves immediately. Unwilling to take the chance that acting at this point would antagonize opinion in the border states which were so important to the Union cause, Mr. Lincoln would not be swayed from his own moderate course. At first as a part of the abolition movement itself, and then in a new organization of their own, Mrs. Stanton and Miss Anthony tried to spur him on.

Their new group was called the Woman's Loyal League, and they formed it because they wanted to make sure nobody missed the fact that women were important to the war effort. But while other women, like Clara Barton and her devoted corps of nurses, took on the more traditional feminine mission of helping the wounded, the woman's rights leaders, being by this time inescapably political-minded, assumed a frankly political role. In effect, they made their organization an arm of the Republican party.

This new party had been born of a merger of smaller anti-slavery political groups, and even though abolitionism was its basic policy, there were still major differences of opinion within Republican ranks. In this case, Mrs. Stanton completely agreed with her husband. She made her new Woman's League an ally of the most radical wing of the Republicans.

Senator Charles Sumner of Massachusetts was a leading spokesman for this faction. Not satisfied that President Lincoln was moving decisively enough, Senator Sumner wanted Congress to seize the initiative by adopting an amendment to the Constitution forever abolishing slavery everywhere in the United States. In order to demonstrate that the public was on his side, he also wanted names, a million names if possible, on petitions urging Congress to act. Furnishing such an unprecedented number of signatures was the task assigned to Susan Anthony. "Here, then, is work for you," Senator Sumner wrote. "Susan, put on your armor and go forth."

During this period, Henry Stanton had moved his family to New York City, so it was from the great metropolis of the North that the Woman's Loyal League scattered its rain of petitions and urgent appeals all the way from Maine to Texas. Through a whole, steamy summer, then all autumn and winter too, Miss Anthony left the Stanton house every morning to go to her cubbyhole office. "Send me the petitions as fast as received," Senator Sumner wrote from Washington. "They give me opportunities for speech."

Miss Anthony scarcely stopped to eat. Two rolls and a glass of milk consumed right at her desk were her lunch, and later she had a dish of strawberries or some other fruit while she sorted through names, stamped envelopes, or otherwise urged on her own small army of volunteers. Nor was her effort in vain. The first sacks of petitions she sent to Washington were so bulky that Mr. Sumner told the Senate he could show them only a token sampling, but he assured his colleagues that he already had more than 100,000 names. Soon the total doubled, then tripled, then nearly quadrupled; in an unmatched example of organizing talent, Miss Anthony gathered nearly 400,000 signatures.

In the spring of 1864 the Senate voted by the required two-thirds majority to adopt Mr. Sumner's anti-slavery amendment; the House of Representatives concurred; the legislatures of sufficient loyal states acted; finally, in December of 1865, when all of the required formalities had been completed, the Thirteenth Amendment, forever abolishing slavery everywhere within the boundaries of the United

States, became part of the supreme law of the land.

By this time, the tragic death of President Lincoln had completely changed the political climate. With his moderating influence removed, the radical wing of the Republican party refused to consider conciliating the defeated South; and as much out of spite as from any sincere interest in helping the free Negro, this group determined to pass another amendment enfranchising former slaves. In the eyes of political opponents, this faction's motive was clear: it seemed beyond question that their main objective was to create a large bloc of grateful Negro voters who would guarantee the success of radical Republican candidates in every national election throughout the foreseeable future.

Being such convinced radicals themselves, Mrs. Stanton and Miss Anthony naturally took quite a different view. To them, the proposed new amendment appeared only simple justice. But being such convinced feminists as well as abolitionists, they also felt an overwhelming excitement at the opportunity opening to them. If the Constitution was to be changed so as to make it a sacred principle of national policy that Negroes should be allowed to vote—*why not women, too?*

More than their own bias convinced them that the question was reasonable. Ever since the first Seneca Falls convention almost two decades earlier, they had been pressing for the ballot, only to be told repeatedly that the country was not ready to consider so radical an innovation. "Thou wilt have hard work," the aging Lucretia Mott had continued to warn Mrs. Stanton; and in her own speeches, Mrs. Mott mildly said: "Far be it from me to encourage women to vote, or to take an active part in politics in the present state of our government." She had been ready to commit herself only to the proposition that women deserved the right to vote, whether or not they chose to exercise the right. But by now

many other women, and some men, had become more accustomed to the idea of women voting. The term "woman
suffrage" was coming into use as the accepted way of referring
to the reform. The notion was no longer such a frightening
novelty.

Furthermore, it seemed obvious that sharp breaks with past
tradition were most likely to take place only after such major
upheavals as the recent war. After the Revolutionary War
there had been a wave of progress, which had almost erased
traditional property requirements for men voters, making the
ideal of universal male suffrage near reality. Indeed the state
of New Jersey had been so heated with enthusiasm over the
Declaration of Independence that for a period of about
twelve years, women had actually been allowed to vote in that
state. Then a scandal arose involving certain females who
stuffed pillows under their skirts to disguise their dimensions,
and thereby gain admission to the polling booth twice on a
single election day. This brought a change in the law.

Following the post-Revolutionary liberalizing wave, there
had been many decades during which the country was too
busy growing to stop and consider electoral reform. But now
another great upheaval had forced attention to the subject of
the ballot, and Mrs. Stanton shrewdly guessed that if woman's
cause were not brought forward now, it might be many years
before another such opportunity arose.

There was another reason which tempted her to raise the
issue in 1866 with all the strength she could command.
Hadn't women earned the favorable consideration of the
Republican party? Surely the brave petition effort by Miss
Anthony and her cohorts entitled women to expect some
thanks, or so it seemed to Mrs. Stanton.

Experienced as she had already become in the strange ways
of politics, she was nevertheless in for a surprise. To her

fervent pleas that woman and the Negro both be enfranchised, she received polite smiles and one answer:

"Be patient. It is the Negro's hour!"

Nor was that the worst of it. During the months of deliberations on the exact wording of the proposed Fourteenth Amendment, many different verbal formulas were tried and found wanting. Earnest abolitionists held out for something more than a pious statement that the vote should not be denied on grounds of race or color; they felt some stronger guarantee was called for if the amendment were not to be winked at in the South. They thought—utterly wrongly, it was soon to be plain—that if the amendment specifically required the population count on which representation in Congress was based to include Negro as well as white citizens, then the intent of the amendment could not be evaded. Most male abolitionists were not ready to allow female Negroes to vote; thus they readily agreed to the inclusion of the word "male" in describing which inhabitants the census should count.

Elizabeth Cady Stanton was aghast.

Up until that time, nowhere in the United States Constitution was the word "male" used to limit eligible voters. Under the doctrine that states alone were responsible for deciding on the qualifications for exercising the ballot, females had indeed been excluded from voting lists. But nothing in the Constitution said this had to be so. Now for the first time, the Constitution could be interpreted to forbid woman suffrage in federal elections. Of course they would fight any such interpretation; but what an effort would be entailed.

"I will cut off this right arm of mine," Susan Anthony stormed, "before I will ever work for or demand the ballot for the Negro and not the woman."

She and Mrs. Stanton found some support for their stand

—but not enough. Even some of their most devoted co-work-ers in past woman's rights struggles deserted them, and urged adoption of the Fourteenth Amendment. "I will be thankful in my soul if *any* body can get out of the terrible pit," Lucy Stone wrote in a letter to one of her abolitionist friends. It was foolhardy to endanger passage of the amendment by fight-ing at this time on the woman issue. But Mrs. Stanton would not agree. She argued with all of her abolitionist friends, in-cluding the same Wendell Phillips who had struck a red-hot iron to her spirit so many years earlier in London when he had refused to do battle on behalf of the women delegates to the world anti-slavery congress. Since then he had recovered her good opinion by staunchly helping her, speaking at her meetings, even raising funds for her cause. Now he forfeited her admiration once more, by refusing to oppose inclusion of that word "male."

"It's the Negro's hour!" he blandly told her.

Weeping with disappointment, Mrs. Stanton wrote to Susan that now they would not see success in their own life-time. Now they would need another Constitutional amend-ment, specifically enfranchising women; or, even harder, sep-arate amendments to every single state constitution. Still, she was too much the optimist to stay disheartened for long. Only a year after almost giving up, she was rejoicing again—at glorious news from the West.

Comes "The Revolution"

7

The rugged Wyoming Territory was noted for its mountains. Fittingly enough, it also had Mrs. Esther Morris. Fully six feet tall, with her other dimensions equally formidable, Mrs. Morris gave somewhat the impression of a walking sculpture representing Mother Earth; even her face had the quality of a granite carving. Owing to this lady's interest in woman suffrage, Wyoming became the first American soil where women were allowed to vote on exactly the same basis as men.

Possibly Mrs. Morris had seemed rather out of place back in upper New York State, whence she had come. Widowed early in life, she had managed to earn her keep in the incongruously dainty work of stitching up stylish bonnets. Then she married a man with three sons, and went West. In the mining camp called South Pass City, she flourished.

But not until 1869, when Wyoming's first territorial election was scheduled, did Mrs. Morris really make her weight felt. Then she called a conclave in her own shack, summoning several respectable women of the area and also some men who were leading political figures. Having once heard Susan

Anthony speak, Mrs. Morris was well prepared. After delivering a competent suffrage lecture, she got down to specifics.

The women of Wyoming wanted the vote immediately, she said.

Was that so? the men murmured uneasily.

We demand the right to vote, said Mrs. Morris. Promise to do something about this!

They promised.

Thus it happened that the territory's first Senate, at its first session a few weeks later, passed the nation's first woman suffrage law. And the governor signed it. The news caused a sensation.

Mrs. Stanton was fifty-four years old and her hair was snowy white, but she capered up and down like a girl; the staid Miss Anthony hugged her young assistants. "It's the beginning!" she exulted. At the same time, cartoonists by the dozen sharpened their pencils and tried to do justice to the possibilities of this ridiculous Western development. Typical of the results was a two-panel drawing. On the left side, ladies in trailing skirts and flower-trimmed bonnets stood in line, looking self-consciously businesslike as they waited to hand in their ballots at a rude frontier polling booth; and on the right side, two gentlemen sat placidly at home in their cabin, one holding a baby on his lap, the other knitting. "This is a reform against nature!" editors stormed.

Despite the storm, Wyoming's new legislators resisted all efforts to repeal their suffrage law, nor did any startling results ensue when Wyoming's women began to vote. Ever since the prospect of feminine balloting had been taken at all seriously, sensible men had predicted horrendous upsets, should the reform be enacted. At the very least, they foresaw a grand conspiracy on the part of the ladies, designed to take over the reins of government and create a veritable chaos.

Woman suffrage in Wyoming Territory. Scene at the polls in
Cheyenne. *Library of Congress*

Political parties would no longer have any reason for existence; every election would be a battle of the women against the men.

But quite to the astonishment of such viewers, it appeared that in Wyoming there were women Republicans, and women Democrats. No appreciable difference in the conduct of public affairs could be discovered after women had cast their ballots in several elections, except that the atmosphere around the polling booths improved considerably. The testimony of a clergyman from Vermont who had only recently come out to Wyoming gave evidence of this.

He wrote home: "I saw the rough mountaineers maintaining the most respectful decorum whenever one of the women approached the polls . . . saying 'Hist! Be quiet! A woman is coming!' And I was compelled to allow that in this new country, supposed to be infested by hordes of cut-throats, gamblers and abandoned characters, I had witnessed a more quiet election than it had been my fortune to see in the quiet towns of Vermont. . . ."

This gentleman also noted that ladies attended by their husbands, brothers, or sweethearts would arrive to deposit their votes "with no more exposure to insult or injury than they would expect on visiting a grocery store or meat market." Indeed, so tranquil was Wyoming's experience that shortly afterward the neighboring Utah Territory followed its lead, becoming the second triumph for the woman's rights forces.

Nevertheless, the struggle was far from over. Had the leaders in the movement foreseen how slow their progress would be, how many separate battles they would have to fight, even their determination might have melted. In all, there were to be *fifty-six* major battles before final victory was won.

Already they had lost the first of these. Kansas, in 1867,

had been the first state to put the question of woman suffrage up to its voters in a special state-wide election. Since only men were presently able to vote, only men were eligible to cast ballots in the special referendum. But there was no law to prevent women from speaking out on the subject, and virtually every prominent feminist from the East had come hurrying toward Kansas.

On a stalled Mississippi steamer, Miss Anthony took advantage of a captive audience by climbing onto a bench and conducting a suffrage meeting; and her enterprising spirit won her a good-natured round of applause, even from convinced anti-suffragists. Mrs. Stanton came along too, although she was very plump by now—she did so like the richest cream in her coffee and fattening pastry of every description.

A lack of good food was only one of the hardships she faced on her tour of Kansas. In a carriage carrying a bushel of suffrage pamphlets, two valises, pails for watering the horses, a basket of apples and whatever other edibles could be bought along the way, she crisscrossed the sparsely settled areas beyond range of railroad lines, speaking in log cabins, unfinished schoolhouses, barns, in the open air, and even in a village mill after working hours were over, by the light of a solitary candle.

Mrs. Stanton was accompanied most of the time by a former governor of Kansas sympathetic to the woman's cause. Going through canyons, fording rivers, often lost, they spent two months on the road; and when these were finished, she had utterly changed her idea of pioneer life. Before then, the West had seemed full of romance. At the sight of covered wagons, she had thought of charming picnics under shady trees, of sleeping wholesomely in the open air. But what she saw in Kansas convinced her the truth was quite otherwise. To the pioneer wife and mother, going West meant an un-

Elizabeth Cady Stanton

Mrs. Stanton.   *National Archives*

finished house, no water for half a mile, malaria and constant fever, and it was a near miracle if her babies lived more than a few months. After her firsthand view of the hard lot endured by pioneer women, Mrs. Stanton thought it no mystery why the women of the West were more easily aroused to fight for their rights than were their Eastern sisters. Lacking all comfort and convenience, they grasped eagerly for the ballot, in the hope of hastening a better day.

But the women of Kansas were not destined to win the vote in 1867. Although suffrage forces mustered the respectable total of nine thousand men in favor of the change, the opposition had sent charges flying thick and fast: that the family as the basic unit of society could not survive woman's enfranchisement; that the authority of men would be completely undermined; that all the fun of life—and most particularly, the pleasure of drinking beer and whiskey—would be forbidden once women could cast ballots. Contradictorily enough, opponents also argued that nice women would never vote, but fast and loose women would. And what sort of prospect was that for the stability of the nation? By enthusiastic use of such arguments, the opponents of woman suffrage amassed twenty-one thousand votes.

Still the Kansas campaign proved of no small importance to the cause of woman. From it came *The Revolution*. This was a newspaper almost as fiery as its name. Even Miss Anthony wondered whether some less frightening title might not attract more readers, but Mrs. Stanton scoffed at the idea. "A journal called The Rosebud might answer for those who come with kid gloves and perfume," she said airily. Growing increasingly radical as she got older, instead of turning safe and sensible, she actually enjoyed shocking polite opinion. It was this adventurous streak that had led her to join forces with the strange individual who put up the money to found *The Revolution*.

She met that eccentric gentleman, a millionaire named George Francis Train, in Kansas. Given to brilliant purple waistcoats and other equally outrageous dress, he was a prominent Democrat who promised to deliver "every Democratic vote in the state" to the suffrage cause. Smarting from what she considered the treachery of the Republicans in connection with the fight over the Fourteenth Amendment, Mrs. Stanton accepted his kind offer.

But the support of Mr. Train was not an unmixed blessing. Being colorful in his habits as well as his clothing, he was laughed at as much as he was heeded. Many other ladies working for woman suffrage shuddered at Lizzie Stanton's indiscretion in accepting help from such a quarter. Still, people did flock to the meetings where he was scheduled to speak, if only to let their own eyes see what he was wearing that evening. Mrs. Stanton could think of no good reason to spurn such a drawing card—particularly when he was so generous with his money.

Why do you not have a newspaper to spread the word about your cause? he asked one day.

Miss Anthony gave the obvious answer that the movement had so much trouble raising funds that it could never pay the bills to start such a paper, helpful as it would surely be.

"Dear, dear," said Mr. Train. "Well, I think I shall have to give you the money myself." And he did. That same evening, he astonished both Miss Anthony and Mrs. Stanton by announcing to his lecture audience that on their return to New York, the two suffrage leaders would begin issuing a new weekly called *The Revolution*—subscription, $2.00; motto, "Men, their rights and nothing more; women, their rights and nothing less!"

While it lasted, *The Revolution* lived up to its incendiary name admirably. The painstaking work of arranging for printing and distribution was handled by Miss Anthony with

her customary efficiency, while Mrs. Stanton, overjoyed at
last to have a regular outlet for her lively pen, contributed
a constant stream of readable articles. Every sort of subject of
special interest to women was discussed, with Mrs. Stanton
delighting in raising sparks from her outspoken words on
such matters as divorce reform, about which no lady was
supposed to speak, let alone write.

But, alas, Mr. Train proved as unreliable as many people
had warned he would be. A hothead on the topic of England's
treatment of the Irish, he took a trip abroad; there his activities were so peculiar as to land him in a lunatic asylum, and
that was the end of any financial support from him. Although
The Revolution had attracted a substantial body of sub-
scribers, their fees were far from sufficient to pay the paper's
expenses. Indeed, when Mr. Train disappeared two and a
half years after *The Revolution* got underway, Miss Anthony
was left with unpaid bills totaling ten thousand dollars. Entirely truthfully, she could have claimed these were not her
personal responsibility; but Susan Anthony, who had rarely
had ten dollars to call her own since she had quit teaching
two decades earlier, simply told the creditors it might take
her some time to do it, but she would pay off every penny.
And she did. By lecturing on woman's rights in any hamlet
where she could find an audience, she earned the sum gradually.

On her travels, someone presented her with a handsome
crimson shawl woven by Indian women. The taste for finery,
which she had once indulged as a young schoolmarm in
Canajoharie, still remained with her, even though since then
she had spent the barest minimum on her own clothing.
Relishing the brightness of the new shawl, she wore it everywhere, and soon it became widely known as her trademark.

Miss Anthony and her red shawl appeared during these

years not merely on small-town platforms. Both became familiar sights in the nation's capital, because the National Woman Suffrage Association, whose guiding genius she was, had its office in Washington and held its conventions there. This dauntless organization was an outgrowth of *The Revolution*.

From the time of the controversy over the Fourteenth Amendment, there had been dissension in the feminist ranks. Miss Anthony and Mrs. Stanton were much too ready to fire off bold statements to suit many of their calmer colleagues. Lucy Stone in particular found them increasingly a trial, and their foolish alliance with Mr. Train—as well as with a bizarre character named Victoria Woodhull, who wanted to run for President—was the last straw. Let them go their way, Mrs. Stone said; she herself would choose another path. Thus the woman suffrage movement split in two in 1869.

Lucy Stone had always tended to be an independent character, and there were those who held that she was really the founder of the woman's rights movement. Born in 1818 on a rocky farm outside West Brookfield, Massachusetts, she was the eighth of nine children. "There was only one will in our home," she later recalled, "and that was my father's." A rosy-cheeked girl with bright gray eyes and silky dark hair, Lucy might have seemed demure enough, but her appearance was deceiving; from her earliest days, she delighted in raising her sweet voice to protest the wrongs suffered by womankind.

Doggedly working as a village teacher to earn the money to pay her own way through the new Oberlin College in Ohio, which accepted girl students, she outraged even the liberal Oberlin by insisting on taking part in college debates. Then on graduating, she serenely informed her parents she intended to become a traveling lecturer. "I expect to plead not for the slave only but for suffering humanity everywhere," she wrote home, and then added in capital letters: "ESPECIALLY DO I MEAN TO LABOR FOR THE ELEVATION OF MY SEX."

Thus by 1848, she was conducting a woman's rights crusade of her own up and down Massachusetts; and two years later, she inspired the calling, in Worcester, of the first woman's rights convention attended by delegates from more than one state. Somewhat grandly, this was termed a national convention, although delegates from only eight states appeared. Nevertheless, it had a great impact—on both sides of the Atlantic. The delicate-appearing Miss Stone, weighing scarcely one hundred pounds and still pink-cheeked and girlish, managed to persuade most of the leading lights in the American reform movement to come address her convention, and as a result the meeting received widespread, even approving, newspaper publicity.

Indeed the favorable accounts published in Horace Greeley's *New York Tribune* circulated as far as London. There the philosopher John Stuart Mill read about the American ladies' revolt—and soon a thoughtful article on the subject appeared in the influential *Westminster Review*. This, in turn, directly stimulated the founding of a woman's rights movement in England, which was to send its own startling ideas crackling back across the ocean when they were needed most.

After the Worcester meeting, Lucy Stone worked along with Mrs. Stanton and Miss Anthony, she wore bloomers with them, she did her share of writing, speaking, traveling. But on her travels, she captured the heart of a man accustomed to strong-minded women. Henry Blackwell, brother of Elizabeth, the first American woman doctor, told Lucy she reminded him of his sister. Short, plump, not a very romantic figure, Henry still managed to win Lucy by promising she would never have to give up her cause for the sake of marriage; indeed he made enough money from his real estate investments so that he could join her often in the good work. They were married in 1855, to the immense amusement of many who marveled at Mr. Blackwell's published statement encouraging his wife not to take his name.

Yet marriage did change Lucy Stone. Surprisingly, to Mrs. Stanton, Mrs. Stone enjoyed housekeeping chores, she doted on her baby daughter, she bemoaned the sad fact that she was unable to have any more children. More and more she stayed close to her comfortable home in Boston, where her husband's business interests had made them settle. Well before *The Revolution,* Mrs. Stone and Mrs. Stanton had cooled toward each other.

Their final break agitated many who loved them both. At the age of seventy-six, Lucretia Mott, whose failing health had gradually curtailed her activities, came out of retirement to try to make peace between them. Having only recently lost her beloved James, her strength was not up to the task, though, and she confided to her diary: ". . . I *cannot* enter into it! Just hearing their talk . . . made me ache all over, and glad to come away and lie on the sofa to rest. . . ."

Thus for political and personal reasons, after 1869 Mrs. Stanton and Miss Anthony worked through their National Woman Suffrage Association, while Mrs. Stone and other milder reformers founded their own American Woman Suffrage Association. The distinction between the two groups was confusing to the general public, but of great importance to the course of the crusade they both supported.

Jail?

8

Bright and early on the morning of November 5, 1872, in the city of Rochester, Miss Susan B. Anthony quite openly committed a crime. A few hours later, she confessed:

> Dear Mrs. Stanton:
> Well, I have gone and done it! Positively voted the Republican ticket—straight!—this A.M. at seven o'clock. . . .
> How I wish you were here to write up the funny things said and done. . . . When the Democrats said my vote should *not* go in the box, one Republican said to the other, "What do you say, Marsh?" "I say, put it in." "So do I," said Jones; "and we'll fight it out on this line if it takes all winter."
> . . . I hope you voted too.
> > Affectionately,
> > Susan B. Anthony

Eight years earlier, when General Ulysses S. Grant had been battling the Confederate Army in Virginia, he had sent a bold dispatch to Washington: "I propose to fight it out on this line, if it takes all summer." Now an equally stubborn

Miss Anthony, leading her suffrage forces on a new front, was amused to have General Grant's very words adapted to her own purpose. And there was a peculiar appropriateness in the use of his slogan; for Miss Anthony had just dared to cast a ballot favoring General Grant's election to a second term as President of the United States.

It was a calculated act of defiance that the feminist leader had carefully planned. Was it *really* a crime for a woman to vote? Certainly the editor of Rochester's Democratic newspaper believed it was, and he had obligingly printed for Miss Anthony's benefit a summary of the law stating that any illegal voter "shall be deemed guilty of a crime . . . and be punished by a fine not exceeding $500 or *imprisonment for not exceeding three years* or both. . . ." But backed by a responsible body of legal opinion, Miss Anthony had come to doubt whether this law applied to females. Indeed she actually contended women could not be prevented from voting.

"No State shall make or enforce any law which shall abridge the privileges or immunities of citizens of the United States. . . ." Thus decreed the Fourteenth Amendment to the Constitution, that same hated amendment Miss Anthony had done her best to defeat.

At the time of its drafting, all her ire had been aroused by the inclusion of the word "male" in the clause relating to eligible voters, and she had overlooked something. Was she not a citizen? Did not another clause of this very amendment guarantee her the privilege of voting? In 1872, she determined to test her interpretation of the word citizen—all the way to the Supreme Court, if possible. There was only one way to obtain a court ruling, which might spell immediate and total victory for the woman suffrage movement. That way was to institute a test case, by insisting on casting a ballot. So at her instigation, several dozen women in various areas audaciously presented themselves at polling places. But it was the case of the United States of America vs. Susan B. Anthony that attracted the greatest interest everywhere.

Not that she was arrested immediately. For several weeks after Election Day, debate raged in the newspapers over what ought to be done about Miss Anthony's brash move. Many Democratic editors sputtered that the republic was in danger, and although some Republicans gingerly suggested the lady might have a point, almost universally they hoped she would not press it any further. Even President Grant himself reportedly was puzzled over how to deal with these determined women; technically, some of his advisers told him, the mere act of voting, when performed by a female, violated a federal law passed in connection with the Fourteenth Amendment. But would it not be more dignified—and perhaps safer on legal grounds—to allow individual states to do as they would? For there was some dispute concerning the constitutionality of the law in question, it being widely held that all regulation of the conditions of voting rightfully fell within the province of the several states.

General Grant apparently was not convinced by this view, however. Nor did he seem to appreciate the compliment paid him by Miss Anthony, whose ballot had not proved at all necessary in ensuring his re-election by a safe margin. The signal came from Washington to the proper federal official in Rochester. On the afternoon of Thanksgiving Day, that gentleman sent an agent to call on Miss Anthony.

Hearing that a visitor had arrived, she came into the parlor of her family's home, where she was met by a tall man in the most irreproachable attire, nervously dandling in his gloved hands a well-brushed high hat. After some incidental remarks, in a hesitating manner he told his mission.

"The commissioner wishes to arrest you," he said.

"Is this your usual method of serving a warrant?" Miss Anthony asked crisply.

Assured that the usual practice was less delicate, she remarked that if she were to be arrested, she chose to be arrested in the normal manner; and no, she would not go by herself to the commissioner's office, she would have to be escorted there.

"Not guilty!" Miss Anthony said, when the charge against her was read a few hours later at a preliminary hearing.

Declining to dismiss the charge, the commissioner ordered her to put up $500 bail so that she could go free until her case came up for trial.

No bail, said Miss Anthony. It did not dismay her in the slightest that unless she put up the money, she would have to wait in jail for her trial. She knew that once there, the legal technicality in the Fourteenth Amendment would make it possible to petition for immediate consideration of her case by the Supreme Court.

But her own attorney overruled her. Chivalrously refusing to allow her imprisonment, he arranged for the bail himself. That was a mistake, Miss Anthony told him sadly; now it would be much harder, perhaps even impossible, to get a hearing from the nation's highest court.

Still she made the best of her freedom. It was six months until her trial was scheduled, and a busy six months they were. Besides Miss Anthony herself, fourteen other Rochester women had been arrested for illegal voting, and three male election inspectors had been formally charged with illegally accepting female ballots. The whole affair was indefensible on several counts, she held. In addition to her basic contention that women were citizens and thus legally entitled to vote, she felt there was no possible justification for the might of the federal government being thrown into the issue this way. It smacked of persecution!

So she said time after time every single day, speaking in post offices, in schoolhouses, in every ward of Rochester itself, and in every tiny hamlet of the county in which the city was located. There was method in her tireless talk marathon: she wanted to make sure she reached so many people that when a jury was chosen to hear her case, no panel of jurors could fail to be aware of the larger issues involved.

Miss Anthony's strategy brought results. It shook the United States District Attorney to such an extent that he asked for the impending trial to be moved into another county. And she accomplished something else, too.

Said the *Rochester Democrat and Chronicle:* ". . . If Miss Anthony has converted every man in Monroe County to her views of the Suffrage question, as the District Attorney intimates in his recent efforts to have her case adjourned elsewhere, it is pretty good evidence—unless every man in Monroe County is a fool—that the lady has done no wrong. . . ."

And the *Syracuse Standard* suggested: "Miss S. B. Anthony is sharp enough for a successful politician. . . . She is conducting her case in a way that beats even lawyers. . . ."

No sooner had her trial been scheduled in the neighboring county of Ontario, than Miss Anthony proceeded to stump that area just as thoroughly. Whether moved by sympathy for her cause, or only by her spunk, newspapers applauded. But it was in Ontario County that the United States of America finally brought Miss Susan B. Anthony before the bar of justice on June 18, 1873.

The scene of the trial was Canandaigua, a pretty lakeside village. Outside the Court House, sun sparkled on the lake; while within, the court clerk solemnly droned the indictment:

". . . against the peace of the United States of America and their dignity . . . did knowingly, wrongfully and unlawfully vote . . . the said Susan B. Anthony being then and there a person of the female sex, as she, the said Susan B. Anthony then and there well knew . . ."

Immediately following the reading of the indictment, opening statements were presented by the district attorney and then by the attorney representing Miss Anthony. Witnesses were called, who testified that the defendant had indeed handed in a ballot at the time and place mentioned. But the twelve men serving as the jury were not to have the duty of deciding whether or not a crime had been committed, because the judge assigned to hear the case had already decided the question.

Reading from a statement he had thoughtfully prepared in advance, he told the jury that the law was plain and he alone could decide points of law; they had no choice.

"I therefore direct that you find a verdict of guilty," he said.

Miss Anthony was, of course, stunned. Her lawyer, a respected former judge, protested. Mrs. Stanton raged; "small-brained" was the politest term she could apply to the trial judge. But public opinion in general, and legal opinion in particular, did not react with any such vigor, and so the verdict was allowed to stand.

However, the temper of the country would not have permitted a prison sentence; even those who ridiculed Miss Susan B. Anthony were ready to admit she was no common criminal. Thus the judge set the punishment at a $100 fine, and naturally Miss Anthony refused to pay it. By now, the United States of America seemed willing to allow the whole matter to drop, but it was not to end without one last laugh at the government's expense.

While all of the female offenders in the case were more or

less officially excused from any legal punishment, the law's chivalry did not extend to the gentlemen involved. The three male election inspectors in Rochester who had so far forgot their duty as to accept female ballots were fined $25 apiece, and they were jailed when they declined, on principle, to pay.

"An Outrage!" said the *Rochester Democrat and Chronicle*. TYRANNY IN ROCHESTER was another headline.

But Miss Anthony and her friends did more than merely fume over this absurd turn of events. By communicating privately to one of the few Senators in Washington firmly committed to the suffrage cause, they were able to initiate steps that led, within a week, to an interesting announcement from the White House.

Meanwhile, the ladies did not let the nation forget the plight of the election inspectors. They cooked and they baked and they carried enormous meals every day to those poor prisoners in the City Jail, while newspaper readers everywhere chuckled at the womanly demonstration. The chuckles soon developed into guffaws when a proclamation devoted specifically to the weighty case of the three local election officials was published in Washington: ". . . in view of the peculiar circumstances of their offense, now, therefore, be it known, that I, Ulysses S. Grant, President of the United States of America . . . do hereby grant . . . a full and unconditional pardon."

In a sense, this episode ended an era. Nobody, neither friend nor detractor, could claim that Miss Anthony gave up after losing her case. Yet after her trial she did seem to adjust her sights, and accept the fact that a sudden, decisive turn of events bringing total victory was not to be realistically expected.

She never gave up hoping, though. In 1868, shortly after the Fourteenth Amendment was passed by Congress, an amendment giving women the right to vote had been introduced for the first time. Congressional friends of the cause, always spurred on by Miss Anthony herself, continued to propose such an amendment at intervals. In 1878, a California Senator who had been fully convinced by her arguments laid before his colleagues the following two sentences as a proposed Sixteenth Amendment:

1. The right of citizens of the United States to vote shall not be denied or abridged by the United States or by any State on account of sex.
2. Congress shall have power to enforce this Article by appropriate legislation.

Although the California Senator's name was Sargent, immediately and irrevocably his amendment became known as "the Anthony amendment." But it did not pass. Indeed the measure received such treatment as to draw from Mrs. Stanton the bitter comment that in the whole course of the struggle for equal rights, she had never felt more exasperated than she did when testifying before the Senate committee assigned to hold a hearing on the proposed amendment. The committee chairman utterly disregarded even the elementary rules of politeness; while she spoke, he alternately stretched, yawned, gazed at the ceiling, cut his nails, sharpened his pencils. "It was with difficulty that I restrained the impulse more than once to hurl my manuscript at his head," Mrs. Stanton confessed.

Thus it could not surprise Miss Anthony when the Senate committee recommended against any action, and the Senate as a whole was not even given a chance to vote on the issue. Such slights were nothing new. Two years earlier, in 1876, when the whole nation had celebrated the one hundredth anniversary of the Declaration of Independence, she had done her best to get a place on the program of the festivities in Philadelphia, to call attention to woman's grievances—and had been soundly rebuffed. Then with her old fire, she had marched right into Independence Hall in the middle of a ceremonial address and handed out copies of a new Declaration of Rights for Women, causing great commotion for a few minutes until she marched right out again to hold a rival meeting in Independence Square.

This was exactly the sort of behavior that acutely embarrassed Lucy Stone and her followers. Moderation was the byword in their camp. They wanted women to vote, but they would be satisfied if their daughters or even granddaughters were in the first voting generation; and they saw no excuse for needlessly antagonizing well-meaning people who were not yet convinced of the desirability of the reform. In their *Woman's Journal,* which was published every week in Boston, they continued to offer polite arguments in favor of woman suffrage, and at their annual conventions in various cities around the country they discussed the possibilities of winning over one state or another. It seemed to Mrs. Stone and her friends much more sensible to work on a state-by-state basis, even if this would take many years, than to attempt the feat of converting Congress.

The federal approach still struck Miss Anthony and Mrs. Stanton as the only sound one. Admittedly, it would be difficult to gain enough support to secure favorable Congressional action on a federal amendment; and then, before woman suffrage became the law of the land, the legislatures of two-thirds of the states would have to ratify the amendment. Nevertheless, if this strategy was followed, only a few thousand men would have to be convinced, while hundreds of thousands, even millions, of male voters would have to be convinced if separate referendums on suffrage were held in

every single state. Having devoted so much of her life to organizing and raising money, Susan Anthony was grimly certain it would be a very long time before women had the
organization, and the money, to mount any such enormous
political campaign.

Thus a basic policy difference separated the two camps of
the woman suffrage movement, and hampered effective action. But even had there been no such difference, the decades
after the Civil War were a period to discourage the hardiest
reformer. "The Gilded Age," Mark Twain called these years
when the United States was surging into an industrial giant.
Huge fortunes were being made almost overnight by oil,
steel, and railroad barons, and so many people were so busy
making money, and spending it on monstrously gaudy gew-
gaws of houses, that very little time or energy was left for
moral issues.

Indeed, political morality was at a remarkably low level.
This was the era when a Boss Tweed could take over New
York City and gleefully steal millions in tax money to buy
the votes of illiterate immigrants, and to line his own pockets
and those of his cronies. It was the era when even solid
citizens would shrug at such goings-on and say with a cynical
smile that human nature had its weaknesses. It was not an era
disposed to be much interested in earnest, high-minded
ladies, many of them quite elderly, who kept repeating almost
plaintively that truly women deserved the right to vote.

In 1887, the Anthony amendment did finally come before
the entire Senate for the first time, and was ably defended by
several Senators, notably Joseph N. Dolph of Oregon.

SENATOR DOLPH: Mr. President, the movement for
woman suffrage has passed the stage of ridicule. . . .

SENATOR GEORGE G. VEST OF MISSOURI: I am not here to

ridicule. . . . But for my part, I want when I go to my
home—when I turn from the arena where man contends
with man for what we call the prizes of this paltry
world—I want to go back to the earnest, loving look
and touch of a true woman. Instead of a lecture upon
finance or the tariff, I want those blessed, loving details
of domestic life. . . .

SENATOR JAMES B. EUSTIS OF LOUISIANA: Women are required to serve on juries in the Wyoming Territory
because they are allowed to vote. . . . Now I ask the
Senator whether he thinks it is a decent spectacle to
take a mother away from her nursing infant and lock
her up all night to sit on a jury?

SENATOR DOLPH: The Senator from Louisiana is a
lawyer, and he knows very well that a mother with a
nursing infant, that fact being made known to the
court, would be excused. . . .

But despite the best efforts of Senator Dolph and a small
band of like-minded men, when the question of woman suffrage was put to a vote in the United States Senate on
January 27, 1887, the tally showed only sixteen yeas—and
thirty-four nays. For one reason or another, twenty-six Senators were recorded merely as absent.

Nevertheless, women were gaining other rights. Under
its gilded veneer American society had many levels, and in
colleges and universities the path was increasingly smooth for
women students seeking admission. Women physicians and
lawyers became less of a rarity, women teachers were taking
over the grade schools. In numerous states, codes of law were
changed to give women the legal right to sign contracts. A
gingerly start was made toward protecting the rights of the
ever-growing army of women factory and office workers. And
in some states, new political as well as economic rights were
being granted.

Often enough to cease causing comment, cities and towns were letting women vote in elections for school board members, or even for members of the municipal council. Though the thought of a woman serving on such a body was still considered outlandish, a few women did win election or appointment to local boards concerned with schools or charity or children. And even on the fundamental issue of full suffrage, there were some encouraging signs.

In 1890, that issue burst into the headlines again. When the Wyoming Territory petitioned for full statehood, women had already been voting there for twenty years, and the proposed constitution for the new state included a woman suffrage clause. Could such a thing be allowed? Many in Congress thought not, and said so heatedly during the debate following receipt of Wyoming's petition. Various irate gentlemen pointed out that not only did women vote in Wyoming, but also they served on juries—this having been considered logical because lists of prospective jurors were taken from the voting lists. Suppose a woman emboldened by voting and by jury duty should actually take it into her head to run for Congress? The monumental Mrs. Esther Morris, in the first known case of a woman on the judicial bench, had been appointed Justice of the Peace in South Pass City. If this Mrs. Morris, for instance, managed to be elected and sent to Washington, how in heaven's name would she be addressed? As Mrs. Congressman?

In an effort to bolster the anti-feminist arguments, several Boston newspapers printed an interview with "a prominent gentleman" from Wyoming, alleging that every evil feared by opponents of woman suffrage had indeed come to pass there since the enfranchisement of females. Nonsense! said Boston's suffrage ladies. And they sent a telegram to the mayor of Cheyenne, asking for particulars about the "prominent gentleman." Came the reply: "A horse thief convicted

Susan B. Anthony and Elizabeth Cady Stanton working on their history of woman suffrage.   *Library of Congress*

by a jury half of whom were women."

This did help the cause, and so did a message from the Wyoming legislature: "We will remain out of the Union a hundred years rather than come in without the women." By a margin of only twelve votes, the House of Representatives at last voted to accept Wyoming with its women; it took the Senate three more months, but finally on June 27, 1890, it, too, capitulated.

Susan Anthony was now seventy years old and Mrs. Stanton almost seventy-five. This was their biggest reward after nearly forty years of pleading, and they made the most of it. They exchanged jeweled pins in the shape of a flag; on the flags there was a single star—for Wyoming, the first suffrage state. "Soon there'll be more!" Mrs. Stanton exulted, ever the optimist.

In the same year of 1890, there was something else for them to celebrate. After twenty years, the split in the woman suffrage movement was finally healed. Old grievances no longer rankled as they had, so the peace overtures initiated by Mrs. Stone's daughter succeeded. The National Woman Suffrage Association and the American Woman Suffrage Association combined to form the National American Woman Suffrage Association. When Lucy Stone, who was also past seventy, joined Miss Anthony and Mrs. Stanton on the platform, and the three old ladies embraced each other, handkerchiefs throughout the meeting hall were touched to tearful eyes. It was an emotional moment, and also a sobering moment. How much longer could these indomitable ladies last?

Mrs. Stone was the first to depart; after gradually failing for many months, she died on October 18, 1893. Although Mrs. Stanton continued remarkably active, jaunting off to Europe to visit a married son and daughter when she was past eighty, she gave up any regular effort on behalf of suffrage soon after the merger, preferring now to devote herself to various quirky writings, in particular a lengthy commentary on the role of women in the Bible. That left only Miss Anthony—but Susan Anthony seemed as if she might be planning to go on leading the suffrage cause forever.

In 1893, her little jeweled suffrage flag acquired another star—for Colorado; in 1896, two more stars—for the states of Utah and Idaho. Nobody knew better than Miss Anthony at what cost the four bright little stars had been won, or how many disappointments there had been along the way, how many campaigns in other states had failed. Yet even as she approached the age of eighty, she was not discouraged. It was 1900, a new century was opening, surely the cause would triumph in this new century, no matter if she did not live to see it. At the annual suffrage convention that year, which had been timed to coincide with a celebration of her own birthday, Miss Anthony stepped forward, clad in soft black satin with lace at the neck and sleeves, and with her famous red shawl over her shoulders.

"I was elected assistant secretary of a woman suffrage society in 1852," she started, speaking almost as firmly as in that distant past. "From that day to this, I have always held an office. I am not retiring now because I feel unable, mentally or physically, to do the necessary work, but because I wish to see the organization in the hands of those who are to have its management in the future. I want to see you all at work, while I am alive, so I can scold if you do not do it well. . . ."

"At this moment," the *Washington Star* reported, "half the women in the hall were using their handkerchiefs on their eyes and the other half were waving them in the air."

Indeed the whole nation took note of Miss Anthony's retirement. Even those editors who still scoffed at woman suffrage did so in a restrained way, and most were ready to admit that the day was bound to come when all women would vote. Whatever their views on suffrage were, their attitude toward Miss Anthony herself was similar. Her single-hearted devotion to her cause over half a century had won for her personally an enormous reservoir of respectful admiration throughout the United States. Rarely had any public figure lived to bask in such praise as was showered on Susan Anthony during her last years.

And when, at the age of eighty-six, she died, the tributes poured forth. On the front page of the *San Francisco Bulletin* for March 3, 1906, there appeared the following:

> GREATEST WOMAN PRODUCED BY NEW WORLD LOST WITH PASSING OF MISS ANTHONY
> Miss Susan B. Anthony, the greatest woman of her century and probably the greatest woman the world ever produced, died at her home in Rochester this morning. . . .

The
Wild Women
of
England

========

9

"What a pity!" exclaimed Mrs. Emmeline Pankhurst, an Englishwoman given to wearing large, floppy hats. "What a pity that great woman won't see the success of her crusade!"

Mrs. Pankhurst's two daughters, Christabel and Sylvia, knew precisely whom their mother meant. Only seven years earlier, in 1899, they had all three shared the thrill of meeting Miss Susan Anthony and of hearing her speak. The famed American visitor had then been almost eighty but had seemed more than equal to keeping a schedule that would have taxed a much younger person. Although the purpose of her trip had been to preside at a London conference of the International Council of Women, which she had been instrumental in creating, she had also found the time and energy to come up to the industrial city of Manchester in the north of England, where the Pankhursts had met her.

It was no mere tourist impulse that had brought Miss Anthony to Manchester. With its blackened brick factories and smoky air, Manchester was undeniably one of the world's ugliest cities, but it was also one of the most reform-minded. When the first word of the American woman's rights movement had crossed the ocean nearly half a century earlier, no other English town had paid as much attention as Manchester did. As early as the 1860's, there was active woman suffrage agitation here; in 1866, nearly four thousand women had turned out to cast ballots in a mass test of the law denying them the vote. The ladies had lost their case in court, but many of them continued to press for a change in the law.

Mrs. Pankhurst had attended her first Manchester suffrage meeting as a girl of fourteen, and in the years that followed she never weakened in her support of the cause. She had married a lawyer known as a convinced suffrage advocate; and while Christabel and Sylvia were still in their cradles, Mrs. Pankhurst was on the executive committee of the local woman suffrage society.

But not until Miss Anthony came to town had Mrs. Pankhurst really taken fire. Almost instantly, she and Christabel and Sylvia resigned from the established suffrage society, which they felt had grown too stuffy over the years, and they founded their own new group, the Women's Social and Political Union. "Deeds not words!" was their motto. By 1905, they had members in several cities—and a plan.

Whether even Miss Anthony herself would have been shocked by the Pankhurst strategy was a question that could never be answered. Because, in one of the fine ironies of history, the special set of circumstances needed to put the new plan into practice occurred just about the time of her death.

For nearly twenty years, England's Conservative party had been firmly in power. And the Conservatives scarcely deigned to recognize woman suffrage as an issue, let alone to sponsor legislation introducing the reform. By 1905, the Liberals, then the other major British political group, were almost desperate to regain control of the government. What Mrs. Pankhurst proposed was nothing less than to force the Liberals to support woman suffrage—as the price of their return to power.

But how could non-voters, no matter how determined, *force* a political party to do anything? Ah! said Mrs. Pankhurst, where there was a will there was a way!

The first clue concerning what she had in mind came during 1905, when the suffrage camp did succeed in getting a suffrage bill introduced in Parliament. As might have been expected, however, the measure was immediately sidetracked, and gentlemen in both parties thought they had solved a slightly troublesome question neatly by choosing to discuss instead a bill requiring drivers of carts to display lights on their vehicles both fore and aft.

These gentlemen underestimated Mrs. Pankhurst. While they debated about carts and lights, a small swarm of women descended on Parliament Square. Mrs. Pankhurst stood up on an upended box to start a protest meeting. Aghast at such effrontery, police dispersed the ladies. Nevertheless, London's newspapers had to take notice of the scandalous episode, and that was only the beginning.

Shortly afterward, a big Liberal rally was held in Manchester. As was customary, one of the party's leaders was describing the program of new laws the party itself would sponsor, should it win power, when a young woman in the audience stood up.

"If the Liberal party is returned to power, will they take steps to give votes to women?" Christabel Pankhurst asked.

A man sitting near her instantly pushed her down. The impudence of the female to interrupt a political meeting!

Amid a babble of hooting and shouting, Christabel stood up again and repeated the question. Another lady stood up on a chair and demanded: "Will the Liberal government give votes to women?" Various men, including Mr. Winston

SAFEST AND CHEAPEST TRAVELLING IN LONDON.

English cartoon depiction of a suffragette and a bobby.

New York Public Library

Churchill, did their best to restore order, but the meeting refused to calm. Christabel and several other young women were dragged out to the street, where they immediately started to ask their question again. Then they were arrested.

Charged with obstructing the street, Christabel was sentenced to pay a fine of five shillings or go to jail.

"You have done everything you could," said Mrs. Pankhurst to her daughter. "I think you should let me pay your fine and take you home."

"Mother," said Christabel, "if you pay my fine I will never go home."

So Christabel and another young woman went off to jail, causing a sensation throughout England. No such wild behavior on the part of females had ever before occurred, newspaper editors told their readers; and newspaper readers wrote letters to editors demanding to know what had gone wrong with the upbringing of the younger generation to account for this terrible flouting of tradition.

"If any argument were required against giving ladies political status and power, it has been furnished in Manchester," a leading political figure pronounced.

Nevertheless, Christabel and Sylvia and their mother were all immensely cheered to hear that the wife of the very speaker Christabel had interrupted was telling friends she thought the girls were quite right. Indeed, by the time Christabel was released from jail, she had become a heroine to a good number of like-minded females.

From then onward, whenever a Liberal meeting was held almost anywhere in England, the air crackled with tension. Would those dreadful suffragettes turn up? More often than not, they did. Despite the utmost in advance precautions, no matter if halls were searched thoroughly beforehand and no females admitted when a scheduled meeting started, sud-

denly a few girls would lower themselves from the rafters—
and unfurl "Votes for Women" banners. Even in London's
Royal Albert Hall, where Scotland Yard itself was in charge
of guarding a great Liberal rally against female interruption,
a girl disguised herself as a man and smuggled in calico banners. The minute the main speaker rose, she whipped them
out and began waving them.

"Will the Liberal government give women the vote?" she
asked in a sweet voice. There was an instant of gasping
silence, then uproar.

"This was the beginning of a campaign the like of which
was never known in England, or, for that matter, in any other
country," Mrs. Pankhurst wrote complacently.

And she was absolutely right. During the next several years,
she and her "wild women"—as respectable opinion described
them—staged one startling coup after another. The Liberals
did win power, but their leadership was not disposed to sponsor suffrage reform, and the party's unyielding policy stirred
increasing militancy among increasing numbers of women.
From merely heckling at meetings, they proceeded to harry
Prime Minister Sir Henry Campbell-Bannerman in person.
Whenever that gentleman stepped out of his official residence
at 10 Downing Street, a cordon of police surrounded him, to
protect him from the women.

A young Irishman named George Bernard Shaw took note
of the bizarre situation. Writing one of his first plays, a
comedy called *Press Cuttings—A Topical Sketch,* Shaw had
the scene open on the commander-in-chief of Britain's army,
seated at his writing table in his London office, opening letters. Suddenly, a voice outside cries: "Votes for women!"
The general starts convulsively, snatches a revolver from a
drawer, and listens in an agony of apprehension. Then a lady
slips in through the open French window. But all at once the

general looks relieved and puts his revolver away. For he recognizes that the supposed lady is really the Prime Minister of England, in disguise. Somewhat petulantly, the Prime Minister explains that this is the only way he has been able to think of to get from Downing Street to the War Office safely.

Utterly disregarding conventional notions of what was and was not ladylike behavior, Mrs. Pankhurst and her women even stormed Parliament itself; fifty-seven women, including Christabel again, were arrested.

The magistrate lectured them: "Such episodes must cease."

"The scenes can be stopped in only one way," said Christabel.

To reinforce the point, Mrs. Pankhurst organized suffrage parades. Bands of small boys and even men threw barrages of rotten oranges and dirty snowballs at the marchers, but still they marched. "Their staying power is extraordinary," the London *Tribune* admitted grudgingly. Then to answer the objection that only a very small number of women really wanted to vote, Mrs. Pankhurst took a bold gamble and announced she would hold the biggest outdoor meeting London had ever seen, on a Sunday afternoon in Hyde Park, London's traditional protest center. By now, she was sure she had mass support, and her confidence proved justified. On the appointed Sunday, streams of determined ladies in long skirts, carrying suffrage banners, converged on the park, filling it with a throng estimated at *two hundred and fifty thousand*. From twenty separate speaker's stands, suffrage leaders shouted a message that triumph must certainly come soon. Even the most anti-suffragist newspapers admitted this was the largest crowd ever assembled in London.

But still the Prime Minister would not relent. "Pay no attention to these cats mewing," some of his cabinet told him. And so Mrs. Pankhurst went one step further. In the summer of 1908, two ladies marching in protest outside of 10 Downing Street took the occasion when the police guard was being changed to reach into the pockets of their skirts and take out handfuls of stones. In an instant, the Prime Minister's house had several broken windows.

Now even some former supporters of Mrs. Pankhurst were horrified, but that lady was not fazed. "Window-breaking when Englishmen do it is regarded as an honest expression of political opinion," she said calmly, and added she saw no reason why the same offense by Englishwomen should be treated as a crime.

Of course it was. But despite the jailing of the offenders, other ladies began throwing stones. At half past five one Friday afternoon in 1909, Mrs. Pankhurst and three other women rode in a taxi to 10 Downing Street, emerged from the cab, threw a stone apiece, and broke four windows; as expected, they were immediately taken to the police station. At quarter to six, another group of ladies emerged from a taxi in Piccadilly Circus and smashed their quota of windows; then fifteen minutes later, the same thing happened on Regent Street; then Bond Street. In all, two hundred women were arrested on what the newspapers called "Black Friday."

Said Mrs. Pankhurst: "We have tried meetings and processions, we have tried demonstrations, all to no avail, and now at last we have to break windows. I wish I had broken more."

But what did Mrs. Pankhurst think could be accomplished by property damage? Several years earlier, when the heckling campaign had just started, she had explained. "What good does it do?" she said. "For one thing, it has made woman suffrage a matter of news. Now the newspapers are full of us.

Mrs. Emmeline Pankhurst, under arrest, being carried by an officer.   *United Press International Photo*

For another thing, we are waking up old suffrage associations, bringing various groups of nonmilitant suffragists back to life. Surely it is something to have inspired all this activity." Clearly she still believed militancy was serving these purposes, even when militancy was pushed to the point of outright disregard for law, as in the case of the window-breaking.

Naturally, a great many people disagreed with her. Indeed, public opinion in Britain was so shaken by the "Black Friday" stone-throwing that magistrates meted out stiff nine-month prison sentences to every offender. Furthermore, the ladies were not to be treated as political prisoners, confined in a special area and given various privileges forbidden to common criminals, as they had expected. Instead they were assigned cells in several of London's oldest jails, and separated, so that each stone-thrower shared quarters with the lowest and most unsavory female offenders.

The response of the suffrage prisoners was dramatic. By a mysterious sort of grapevine, they communicated with each other in their separate cells. Then on the same day, they each and every one refused to swallow a bite of food, in protest against their jailers' tactics. It was a mass hunger strike.

No such shocking maneuver had been anticipated by the authorities, and they could not decide how to cope with it. Day after day, Mrs. Pankhurst and all the rest who were behind bars steadfastly and inflexibly refused to eat. Their physical strength swiftly ebbed, but their will power seemed dauntless. In the face of mounting public outcry, high government officials finally acted. The only known method of forcible feeding then was extremely painful and unpleasant; deciding they had no choice, the leaders of the government ordered that each hunger striker be forcibly fed.

No matter that the women had brought their suffering on themselves, protest messages poured in from many directions.

Even in Parliament, which had been so strong for punishing the women, voices were raised demanding to know if the punishment in this case really fit the crime. Were the women not being persecuted ignobly?

On the other hand, there were those who insisted the government must not back down. How could a decent respect for law and order be maintained if lawbreakers were pampered?

Faced by what it felt was a terrible dilemma, the government tried a new tack. Relenting, but only partially, it released the women in groups of two or three—temporarily. As soon as medical testimony could be presented certifying that the paroled prisoner had regained her health, the lady would again be clapped into jail. "A cat and mouse game!" Mrs. Pankhurst said scornfully.

Then when her turn came, and she was released from her cell, she defied the warning that she was still technically a prisoner, and she sailed off—on a lecture trip to America.

To the Rescue!

10

Something had been happening gradually to the American woman suffrage movement. While Susan Anthony still lived, the plain truth escaped notice mainly because of the force of her personality and the esteem in which she was held. But rather than growing ever stronger, her cherished cause was instead sinking—sinking deeper and deeper into a rut.

New ideas, new slogans, new tactics, were desperately needed for the new twentieth century. Yet an air of old-fashioned quaintness seemed to have settled down over the whole subject of woman's rights. An energetic high school principal from Iowa named Carrie Chapman Catt had taken over leadership of the movement in 1900, when Miss Anthony retired, but even the enormously capable Mrs. Catt did not appear to know how to cope with the aging, tired organization she inherited. It was so beset by cranky quarrels among its board members, and a listless disinterest in departing from routine, that when her husband's health became a problem in 1904, Mrs. Catt almost gratefully gave up the struggle and resigned her post.

Her successor was Dr. Anna Shaw, both a minister and a

Carrie Chapman Catt. *League of Women Voters*

doctor, and a stirring platform speaker; but as an organizer, her talents were sadly limited, and under her administration the National American Woman Suffrage Association did hardly more than flounder along the same old track.

Nor did the various state suffrage societies provide a much brighter picture. In some Western states, it was true, spirited efforts continued to be made. Oregon, for instance, had a dauntless group that kept trying to add a suffrage amendment to the state constitution; but even Oregon's convinced feminists proved in 1906 that old-fashioned arguments were not enough to win with.

Suddenly, a few weeks before the scheduled suffrage referendum that autumn, a torrent of postcards flooded the mails in Portland. These were eye-catching cards, anonymously printed. Each was adorned by a drawing of a female undergarment. "NO PETTICOAT GOVERNMENT!" said the terse message beneath the picture.

Before such an attention-catching onslaught, the suffrage ladies were helpless. They issued pious statements to the newspapers: "The scurrilous card bearing a picture of a woman's undergarment is a sample of the lowest political scheming that has disgraced the state of Oregon," they said. "It is not only an insult to Oregon womanhood, but a reflection on the honor of Oregon manhood as well." But alas, for every ten men who grinned at the silly drawing, there probably were not even one or two who even troubled to glance at the ladies' irate statements.

The women's wrath was further compounded when they learned the source of the cards. It was "The Hidden Enemy!" This melodramatic term referred to the liquor interests, and it did seem an apt name. It was undeniably apparent that a local association of beer brewers and liquor wholesalers had paid for distribution of the petticoat cards. But why?

Because they were afraid of the woman's vote. They were convinced that once women had a say about making laws, a law prohibiting all sale of alcoholic beverages would immediately be passed. And not only the liquor industry was possessed of this idea—from the farmer whose corn was used for making whiskey to the saloon-owner who sold the finished product; the notion had been firmly established in the mind of the general public, too.

There was some reason for the prevalence of the fear that woman suffrage would inevitably bring prohibition in its wake. Among the earliest feminists, most if not all had been infuriated by the bland insistence of existing law that a husband, no matter what his faults, had full control of his wife's property and person; and since by far the most common fault among American men of the time was drunkenness, most suffragists were also dedicated temperance supporters. Like Miss Anthony herself, many other suffrage workers had started their reform careers in the temperance movement.

Throughout the years there had been a certain overlapping in the membership of suffrage and temperance societies. Yet the connection was never as close as some people thought it was. Under the shrewd leadership of Miss Frances Willard, the Woman's Christian Temperance Union had spread from the Midwest to become a powerful force in the South as well; and suffrage had never been able to win any substantial following in the chivalrous South. Although Miss Willard herself had grasped Miss Anthony's point that political rights—particularly, the right to vote—would vastly improve woman's ability to influence lawmakers, and although Miss Willard had sought for years to add her organization's strength to the suffrage cause, she had not succeeded notably. For temperance was less radical, and more respectable, than suffrage; and also more popular. By 1900, the W.C.T.U. had ten times the membership of suffrage societies, including numerous sternly religious ladies who shuddered at the forwardness of the bold females demanding the ballot.

Thus suffrage had failed to profit from the rapid growth of the temperance movement, and, in fact, had actually suffered from it. For, as temperance societies grew in strength and were able to push through local, and sometimes even state, laws banning alcoholic beverages, the liquor industry became thoroughly alarmed. It was true that women were more likely than men to vote in favor of prohibition, and therefore, in many cities where widespread support for suffrage might have been expected among educated and progress-minded men, the organized opposition of tavern-owners effectively stifled serious consideration of the subject.

As early as the 1880's, Lucy Stone's husband, Henry Blackwell, had warned that "to link the two questions would be fatal," and, convinced temperance advocate though she was, Miss Anthony herself had tried to keep the two causes separate in the public mind.

It was by no means a fact that adoption of woman suffrage led immediately and automatically to prohibition. This had not happened in Wyoming, where women had been voting since 1869. And in five Southern states, where the prospect for women ever voting seemed dim indeed, state-wide prohibition laws were on the verge of passing at the time of the Oregon suffrage referendum in 1906, and did pass shortly afterward.

Nevertheless, the anti-prohibition propagandists managed in Oregon, by fair means and foul, to convince the majority of the electorate that woman suffrage would surely mean the end of man's freedom to drink so much as a single glass of beer. And the woman suffrage supporters seemed powerless to stop "The Hidden Enemy!" Furthermore, the ladies appeared to be equally powerless in combating their other major enemy. Its name was apathy. Many men simply were not interested enough in the suffrage question to bother registering opinion on it. In a distressingly small turnout of voters, the Oregon suffrage referendum was defeated by a margin of ten thousand.

Nor did any other state do better in this period. It actually seemed to be getting harder, rather than easier, to add even one more star to the flag-shaped lapel pins devoted suffragists wore. As for federal adoption of suffrage, it seemed as remote as ever. Almost every year some obliging legislator introduced the Anthony amendment in Washington—"the pestiferous perennial," one anti-suffrage Senator called it—but pressure for action was so slight that the measure was regularly buried in committee, without even being brought to a vote.

Dire times indeed had befallen the cause. But just when the outlook was at its bleakest, there came charging to the rescue, like some new-fangled feminist version of the brave knight of old, the doughty Mrs. Pankhurst.

Not that the lady personally took over the task of reviving the American suffrage movement. Well before she herself crossed the ocean, word of her exploits had begun doing so. Even in the United States, newspaper writers and cartoonists had gleefully seized on the story of her war with the staid old English Parliament and made it front-page news. If some failed at first to see that there might be American repercussions resulting from what was happening over in England, they quickly learned better.

The first repercussions were quiet and undramatic, and occurred abroad. Mrs. Carrie Chapman Catt was in Europe to help bolster one of Susan Anthony's last enthusiasms, an organization recently renamed the International Woman Suffrage Alliance. Mrs. Catt instinctively disliked such violent demonstrations as the throwing of acid into mail boxes; and the spectacle of women chaining themselves to the railing outside the British Prime Minister's residence at 10 Downing Street made her shake her head in dismay; but there was no denying that these women were accomplishing a great deal. Spurred on by the new, intense public interest in woman suffrage, thousands of other, more reasonable women were being drawn into working for the cause, and success within a comparatively short period of time seemed all but assured. Carrie Catt noted this carefully.

So did another American woman with a name to reckon with in suffragette ranks. She was Mrs. Harriot Stanton Blatch, the daughter of Elizabeth Cady Stanton (who had died peacefully in 1902, at the ripe age of eighty-seven). Mrs. Blatch had married an Englishman and had been living in England for several years. Widowed in 1907, she was ready to go back to the United States—and bring the Pankhurst message with her.

There were also two American college girls who had come to London for further study—and soon were excitedly marching in Pankhurst suffragette demonstrations. Their names were Alice Paul and Lucy Burns. Before Miss Paul returned to Philadelphia, she had earned the pin Mrs. Pankhurst awarded to any of her followers who were jailed for the cause.

In 1907 and 1908, these and other Americans were storing impressions of Mrs. Pankhurst's campaign, or preparing to adapt what they thought best for transplanting across the Atlantic. Numerous other American women who had never left home were avidly reading newspaper stories sent from London, and making plans of their own. And at the same time, various native American forces that might eventually have revitalized the American suffrage movement on their own, also were stirring.

There was, for instance, a new generation of college-trained women, many of them social workers, briskly engaged in try-

ing to improve living conditions in big-city slums. Other
women were organizing women's trade unions. To improve
economic conditions in slums or sweatshop factories, political
power was essential; this new generation did not need "Aunt
Susan" or even Mrs. Pankhurst to tell them that. And
furthermore, they also knew that the only way American
women would ever win the vote would be by converting
substantial numbers of the husbands and fathers of factory
women to the cause.

The necessity for working-class support was a fact of American political life that most of the first, basically "ladylike,"
reformers had refused to recognize. When hordes of immigrants from Europe had begun pouring into the United
States, Mrs. Stanton had bitterly complained over the un-
fairness of giving these "ignorant foreigners" the vote while
educated and respectable American-born women were denied
it. Her outspoken prejudice against "foreigners" had grown
with the years, and most suffrage workers in her generation
felt exactly the same.

Susan Anthony had tried at times to broaden the feminist
base of support by enlisting working women into the battle,
but she had made little headway against the refusal of old-line
suffragists to dirty their skirts among poor people. In short,
the old suffrage movement had been basically a middle-class
movement. But in the first decade of the twentieth century
there were beginning to be signs that the far more numerous
working class might be led to join, too.

At the opposite end of the social scale, among very rich
women and society leaders, a somewhat similar awakening
was occurring. In numbers these ladies may not have
amounted to a significant portion of the population, but their
money and their status gave them an influence far outweigh-
ing their numerical importance. During many decades, Miss
Anthony had been hard put to raise even a few hundred dol-

lars. At Newport and other fashionable resorts, nary a thought was given to woman suffrage, except perhaps to cast a well-bred barb at the vulgarity of the whole idea.

Now, however, suffrage had become socially acceptable. Perhaps because of honest conviction, possibly partly for its novelty appeal, the movement was gaining supporters worth their weight in gold. Mrs. John D. Rockefeller opened her town house for suffrage teas. Mrs. O. H. P. Belmont wrote checks—and made speeches. The cream of New York's "Four Hundred" attended a suffrage reception in the city's most elegant restaurant.

Thus, by 1909, when Mrs. Pankhurst made her first lecture trip to the United States, she found a movement that, although it was still far from lively, was already in a state of flux—to a certain extent because of purely American economic, social, and political currents; possibly to a larger extent because of her own rousing militancy over in England.

"I am what you call a hooligan," Mrs. Pankhurst cheerfully introduced herself to lecture audiences in New York, Boston, Baltimore, Chicago. The shouts of laughter this brought were in themselves refreshing to suffrage supporters. It had been a long time since they had had much to laugh about.

Nevertheless, her visit did not inspire unmixed joy in the American suffrage ranks. Many old-time believers in the cause were so repelled by her militant methods that they joined with conservative newspaper editors in denouncing her. She had actually set the cause back at least a generation by antagonizing respectable opinion, they muttered. Among the dissidents was Dr. Anna Shaw, president of the National Suffrage Association, who refused even to meet Mrs. Pankhurst, for fear the contact would tar the American movement with the taint of British lawlessness.

But by the time Mrs. Pankhurst came back to the United States three years later, she found quite a change. Women decked out with sandwich-style picket signs marched up and down main streets, advertising her meetings. Excitement was in the air. The state of Washington had voted in woman suffrage, and so had California—the largest and most populous prize so far, after a suffrage campaign unmatched in American history for its enthusiasm. During the weeks just preceding the referendum women from every state had suddenly joined exuberantly in the fight.

One headline in the *New York World* read: BEGIN SELF-DENIAL WEEK. Suffragettes Save Money to Help Cause in California.

HATE BEANS, BUT EAT 'EM. By Such Economies, Earnest Women Pour Coins into Party Coffers . . . That was another headline.

More states added stars to the suffrage flag. On Election Day in 1912, Arizona and Kansas voted yes to suffrage. Despite "The Hidden Enemy," so did Oregon—at last. And so, it seemed, had Michigan, although the count in that state was extremely close.

To celebrate, the suffragettes of New York City held a gay torchlight parade almost on the spur of the moment, and drew out several thousand marchers. They stepped smartly to a downtown square where Dr. Anna Shaw herself stood up on a platform and shouted out to the happy throng:

"Fellow Citizens!"

Cheering interrupted her for several minutes until Dr. Shaw could make herself heard again. Sensing that the time had passed for mere speech-making, Dr. Shaw then raised her arms and led her ladies in a jubilant chant: FOUR! FOUR! FOUR STATES MORE!

SUFF
on
the
March

11

The 1912 convention of the National American Woman Suffrage Association met in Philadelphia. Unlike so many of the previous annual meetings, this one had a crackle of excitement about it. Four states had just joined the suffrage ranks, or seemed certain to do so shortly; and in several other states, marvelously revived local societies were mounting campaigns that appeared likely to succeed. Plump Dr. Anna Shaw had never looked more perky than she did presiding at this Philadelphia session.

Still to some of the younger women in the assembly there seemed cause for sober thought. Suppose another four or five states did pass suffrage referendums, then what? The chances for making further progress on a purely state-by-state basis would be extremely slim because many states had constitutions written in such a way that the adopting of any sort of amendment was practically impossible.

Moreover, in a substantial number of other states, any political realist could see that the chances for obtaining a pro-suffrage majority in the foreseeable future were very remote. Virtually the whole of the Deep South fell into this category. So, unhappily, did the industrial East, where big-city political machines had already shown they would fight suffrage every step of the way, even to the extent of tearing up pro-suffrage ballots in the polling districts they controlled. Such tactics had been tried in California, to the horror of female poll watchers inexperienced in the seamy side of American political practice.

It was a compliment to the nation's womanhood that political bosses strenuously opposed woman suffrage; for their opposition certainly seemed to be based on a fear that the woman's vote could not be bought or swayed, and that the ladies might briskly roll up their sleeves and clean America's political house.

Compliment or not, the antagonism of the bosses—and of the uneducated portion of the male electorate among whom their influence was strongest—carried a plain meaning. The conclusion seemed unavoidable that within a few years, most of the women who lived west of the Mississippi River might be voting, while *few, if any, of the women living east of the Mississippi would enjoy the same privilege.*

That is, such an unnatural situation might be expected unless the suffrage movement as a whole did an about-face and began to press Congress hard for passage of the Anthony amendment. In the new climate of suffrage enthusiasm, securing ratification of the amendment by the legislatures of thirty-six states could be considered a reasonable possibility. Beyond question, the chances were better than those for securing a majority vote in favor of woman suffrage from the whole male electorate in forty-eight states.

Thoughtful discussion along such lines had been occupying small groups of younger delegates to the Philadelphia convention for some months before the meeting, but including the topic on the formal agenda apparently had not occurred to the suffrage association's leadership. The new stars on their suffrage flags thrilled these ladies; they spoke up in joyous succession promising each other eventual full success. When would it come? That did not strike them as overly important.

Indeed, not only had they become accustomed to thinking in long-range terms; but also a goodly number were not anxious for any undue haste. Their willingness to wait patiently reflected what they believed to be political wisdom. They did not want to antagonize the Southern membership.

By now, most of the opposition to woman suffrage in the South hinged on race prejudice. It was not just white women who would get the vote, went the muttered argument among the segregation-minded; much worse, Negro women would cast ballots, too. Virtually everywhere in the South, Negro men were being effectively kept from voting by one device or another, despite the clear intent of the Constitution as amended after the Civil War. The anti-suffrage sentiment did not acknowledge this fact, and perhaps some of its bitterness stemmed from concern that a new expansion of the potential voting population would call the whole nation's attention to the widespread disregard for Negro men's voting rights.

As a body, the old-line leadership of the woman suffrage movement did not sympathize with the segregationist prejudice. However, there had gradually come into being a bloc of Southern suffrage societies committed to educating the South over a long period of time to accept suffrage, and opposed to antagonizing the South by seemingly seeking to foist an unwanted reform on it. In deference to these member societies, the board of the National Association had repeatedly reduced its efforts on behalf of the Anthony amendment—until the grand sum of ten dollars was all the annual budget allowed for expenses in connection with putting the case before Congress. The Association no longer even maintained a Washington headquarters; a lady who lived in the capital took it upon herself to call on Senators in their offices from time to time, and the ten dollars repaid her for what she spent on postage and stationery when she wrote for appointments.

Absurd! sputtered various younger suffrage enthusiasts. And at private meetings in Philadelphia hotel rooms, they concocted a scheme.

Thus it happened that Dr. Shaw received a visit from two young women toward the end of the convention, while committee assignments for the ensuing year were being prepared. They wished to volunteer to set up a new committee in Washington, they told her respectfully. Their aim would be to persuade Congress to hold hearings on the Anthony amendment. As far as expense was concerned, they told her, the Association need have no worries because they intended to raise whatever money they needed, and thus would not drain away any funds from other programs. Dr. Shaw thanked the young women for their generous offer, then asked time to consider it. She hesitated because she had recognized their names. They were Alice Paul and Lucy Burns.

It disturbed Dr. Shaw that the two had been in England, and had marched with Mrs. Pankhurst. Above all, Dr. Shaw wanted no wildness in her ranks. Over in England, those terrible Pankhursts were now ravaging the countryside, setting fire to golf greens, on the theory that men had no right to play games while women were deprived of the right to vote. It appalled Dr. Shaw to contemplate such lawless militancy, and she questioned the two volunteers carefully concerning their attitude toward the Pankhurst tactics.

Miss Paul reassured her. There was no reason for militancy in America, she said. With state after state accepting suffrage, Congressmen would be willing to listen politely to the arguments for a national amendment.

Yes, indeed, said Miss Burns. Presenting the facts of the case was all they planned.

Dr. Shaw heard them out and then decided that certainly the two young women seemed to have settled down. They made a respectable impression; one had become a high school teacher, the other a social worker. Encouraged by a few of her more adventurous board members, especially Miss Jane Addams, the noted social worker from Chicago, Dr. Shaw agreed to the establishment of the new committee.

For the next few months she had no reason to repent of her decision. No frightening news arrived from Washington. Indeed, the only word concerning the new committee listed four additional members, each eminently respectable; one was the wife of a California Congressman, another the wife of a history professor. Since a national election campaign was underway, in which a new President and a new Congress were being chosen, the lack of activity was only to be expected. Nevertheless, the silence on the Potomac front was taken as evidence that really nothing had changed—that the crucial areas in the battle for woman suffrage were still the various states where referendum campaigns were being planned.

Miss Paul proved to be merely biding her time. No sooner was Election Day past than she began organizing her first coup. Scholarly Woodrow Wilson of Princeton had just given the Democratic party its first President since Grover Cleveland; and on the day before his inauguration, the energetic Miss Paul gave Mr. Wilson, and the whole United States, a foretaste of things to come. Arriving in Washington that day, Mr. Wilson was puzzled by the lack of people in the streets along his route. Where were they? he asked. Over on Pennsylvania Avenue, he was told, watching suffragists parade.

Five thousand strong, Miss Paul's marchers started down the avenue in a demonstration shrewdly planned to take advantage of the fact that the capital was filled with visitors for the morrow's inauguration festivities. Even had there been no trouble, the parade would surely have caused talk. But there was trouble—and it turned suffrage into a sensation.

Having been well trained in the mechanics of organizing mass protests, Miss Paul had gone through the proper channels to obtain a police permit for the parade. So what happened was not really her fault. The police had been forewarned of the demonstration—and neglected to take the necessary steps. No special details of men were deployed along the marching route. Thus it was easy for rowdies in the sidewalk crowds to erupt into violence.

Banners were whipped out of the women's hands and torn to shreds. Members of the presumably frailer sex were pushed, shoved, jeered at. If various detachments of soldiers, including a troop of cavalry from nearby Virginia, had not been rushed to the scene, the unruly "spectators" would almost certainly have caused serious injuries.

Reported the *Baltimore Sun* of March 4, 1913: "The women had to fight their way from the start and took more than one hour in making the first ten blocks. Many of the women were in tears under the jibes and insults of those who lined the route. . . . Few faltered, though some of the older women were forced to drop out from time to time. . . ."

"No inauguration," said the *Baltimore American* of the same date, "has ever produced such scenes, which in many instances amounted to nothing less than riots."

Apart from whatever feelings they had about the suffrage issue, people all over the country were so shocked by the spectacle of violence on the streets of their national capital that an official inquiry was immediately held. Washington's police chief was fired. Beyond any possible advance predictions, the parade succeeded in bringing woman suffrage onto America's front pages. And there it stayed.

For a good many headline writers, "SUFFRAGE," with its eight letters, took up too much space. So they blithely abbreviated it to "SUFF." Only the most important people and

Suffrage gets rolling.   *The New York Times*

happenings were honored by such familiar treatment. When the nickname blossomed on newsstands everywhere, it was a clear sign that the cause had arrived as a major issue.

Capitalizing on the tremendous sudden interest in suffrage, action-minded "suffs" in many states went to work with a will. Automobiles were bought and draped with gaudy suffrage banners. Cavalcades of cars from as far away as California set out toward Washington. With a honking of horns, a ringing of cowbells, even the tootle of trumpets by lady trumpeters newly enlisted in the cause, sleepy towns all over the map were roused to turn out for a curbside suffrage meeting. Nor was the aim of such activity merely to keep national attention on suffrage, although that was part of the purpose. But inspired by Miss Paul, the delegations from all over the country were also carrying petitions demanding passage of the Anthony amendment.

On July 31, less than four months after President Wilson had taken office, a motor parade of suffragists drove up to the Capitol and delivered two hundred thousand signatures. Then groups of ladies were directed by Miss Paul to keep appointments with the Representatives of their home states. Meanwhile, other groups went to the White House. There President Wilson, a man not noted for his sense of humor, reportedly said, when asked to give his views on the suffrage issue, that the matter had never been called to his attention.

Miss Paul took ample pains to see that this possible oversight was remedied. She wanted a commitment from the President to support the Anthony amendment, and from the summer of 1912 onward she kept a continuous stream of women bombarding him with appeals. She sent delegations of Western women and Eastern women, of working women and college women, all bearing the same message.

Meanwhile, one of the most intensive lobbying campaigns in American history got underway. Every Senator and Representative was sought out and asked to support hearings on the suffrage amendment. In Washington, and in their home states too, these gentlemen were constantly reminded of woman suffrage; Miss Paul was gradually making her committee bigger and sending agents around the country.

All of this activity could not but make Dr. Shaw uneasy. Nevertheless, for the first year or so she saw no grounds for serious alarm. Imaginative as Miss Paul's methods were, they stayed well within the law. And even the most convinced supporters of the state-by-state policy had to admit the new national effort was not hampering their own work. On the contrary, many states were showing wonderfully increased vigor in campaigning for state-wide referendums. Beyond any doubt now, "SUFF" was on the march, as headline writers kept reporting.

This was literally true. Some years earlier, on her return from England, the brisk Mrs. Blatch—Lizzie Stanton's daughter—had proposed the idea of parading to call attention to the cause. It had proved a splendid idea; Mrs. Stanton would have been proud of her.

Parading was attention-getting, and it was legal. With a police permit, suffrage marchers could take over New York's Fifth Avenue, practically at will, and get their message to tens of thousands of shoppers. The first parades had been small and straggly affairs, bedeviled by sidewalk hecklers. But suddenly the spectacle of banner-toting women by the thousands, wearing distinctive yellow capes, was startling major cities throughout the country, and the curbside crowds were surprisingly friendly, even respectful. Wives and daughters of bankers and bootblacks, of storekeepers and college professors, were all striding along together down the middle of the avenue; with their own womenfolk marching, few men cared to jeer.

Numerous new groups representing teachers or nurses or

some other previously unorganized segment of the female population were combining forces with the old, established suffrage societies to press for the ballot. In this sudden mushrooming of additional strength lay a potential challenge to the old-line leadership. In New York, for instance, Mrs. Blatch had organized her own Women's Political Union, which offered a few distressing parallels to the early program of Mrs. Pankhurst's Women's Social and Political Union. Nevertheless, for the time being there seemed no danger of unpleasantness.

Indeed in Illinois, in 1913, the old and the new suffrage groups cooperated handsomely to score a stirring victory. Because the governor of the state positively refused to authorize a suffrage referendum, even though there appeared to be widespread backing for the reform, the ladies thought up an alternate plan. They decided that the Federal Constitution gave the legislature of each state the power to set qualifications for Presidential electors, and they set about convincing members of the Illinois legislature that women should be allowed to vote for President. Astonishingly, the plan worked. By legislative edict, the women of Illinois were granted the ballot. For the first time, there were women voters *east* of the Mississippi. Efforts were immediately started to extend the Illinois plan to other states, but anti-suffrage forces were not to be caught napping elsewhere, and gradually interest in the scheme dwindled.

Conventional referendum campaigns continued, and in 1914 they were carried on in seven states. However, only in two—Montana and Nevada—did the suffrage cause win. Despite all the enthusiasm and ingenuity mustered for the cause in the other five—the Dakotas, Missouri, Nebraska, and Ohio —the "anti's" proved too powerful, and state-by-state the movement suffered a grievous blow to its prestige. Nevertheless, the ladies were not ready to concede defeat, not at all. In

STOP! LOOK! LISTEN!

Provided you are a live one. If
dead already, stay where you
are and be run over by the

SUFFRAGETTE EXPRESS

That will overtake the fast Male at the

MISSOULA THEATRE

Tuesday evening, February 10, 1914
at 8:30 o'clock

Miss JEANETTE RANKIN
of the Greatest City on Earth,
will act as engineer and introduce:

Mr. James Lee Laidlaw	Mrs. James Lee Laidlaw
of New York, second greatest	of New York City,
city, President of the	chief titles too
National Men's League	numerous to mention
for Woman Suffrage	

Who Will Discourse Eloquently on the
Latest Agricultural Stunt of

Making 2 Votes Grow Where Only 1 Grew Before

Have your life insured and bring your
fire-arms for there are going to be

MANY BOMBS EXPLODED and
MANY BALLOONS PUNCTURED

Admission
Free

COME ONE, COME ALL
COME SEVEN, COME ELEVEN

Admission
Free

TONIGHT! TONIGHT!

Text of poster announcing a Montana suffrage rally. The exuber-
ant campaign there succeeded, and Miss Rankin, who had led the
suffrage forces to victory, was elected to Congress in 1916, becoming the first woman member of the House of Representatives.
Courtesy of the New York Historical Society, New York City

Pennsylvania, New Jersey, Massachusetts, and New York, they were already working hard to win in 1915. If these four could be secured, the implications for the whole country would be enormous.

Mrs. Carrie Chapman Catt had come out of semiretirement to direct the New York drive. Now an imposing woman in her middle fifties, she was proving herself a general to frighten any enemy. As a beginning suffrage worker in Iowa, she had demonstrated an organizing genius that shot her up through the ranks right to Miss Anthony's attention. But Mrs. Catt had first come into national leadership when the suffrage cause was in the doldrums, and even she had seemed powerless. Now, however, she had a revitalized army at her command, and she awed all who beheld her, serenely jotting notes for her "Plans of Action," outlining the biggest political campaign women on their own had ever undertaken anywhere.

Mrs. Catt brought nearly twenty assorted pro-suffrage groups, some large, some small, into a good semblance of unity. If any rivalries developed, she smothered them swiftly. The point was to fight the enemy, not each other, she told her ladies briskly. And they listened. For a time, cartoonists tried to poke fun at the spectacle of rich Mrs. Belmont marching along with Sewing Machine Susie, but they had to give up—because Mrs. Catt's various committees refused to provide ammunition by indulging in any feminine hair-pulling matches.

Furthermore, they all worked like Trojans. Typewriters clicked day and night at headquarters, sending out instructions: "To all district leaders—This is the time for you to do several very definite things. . . ." No detail was glossed over as too small to matter. When an upstate village chairman complained that her local newspaper was edited by a former clergyman violently opposed to woman suffrage, a man who refused to print anything about suffrage meetings, head-quarters dispatched crisp instructions: Arrange to have suffrage speakers stand up at grange meetings, for local papers almost always print full accounts of these, and even if what the suffrage speaker said fails to get into print, the farmers present will hear it.

Money was raised, parades were staged, brass bands blared on street corners to attract crowds for suffrage rallies. More than that, Mrs. Catt kept telling her ladies it was no use merely to talk to other ladies. No, perhaps it was of some use, because the ladies would convince their husbands. But far more important, men—especially men who thought they were not the least bit interested in woman suffrage—had to be reached and convinced to vote for it.

So there were Suffrage Days in New York's barber shops. On these days, teams of attractive young ladies went from barber shop to barber shop, sweetly complimenting barbers on their ability to sway opinion among their clients—and then requesting that with every haircut, there also be dispensed a few words in favor of woman suffrage.

There were also Suffrage Days at the Polo Grounds, when men who had come out to see the New York Giants take on the Chicago Cubs were treated, too, to gay displays of suffrage banners, and a few well-chosen words about suffrage between the innings.

There was also what the newspapers were pleased to call "tele-suffing." That meant spending all day on the telephone saying brightly time after time: "Hello! Do you favor suffrage? We hope you'll vote for it. . . ."

Through all of this, the "anti's" naturally did not remain silent. "DO WOMEN WANT THE VOTE?" a new organization known as the National Association Opposed to Woman Suffrage demanded in leaflets strewn all over New York State. The answer, they claimed, was a resounding negative. Books with titles like *The Wrongs and Perils of Woman Suffrage* were distributed. From New England, a group describing itself as the Massachusetts Association Opposed to the Further Extension of Suffrage to Women entered the fray. Composed of well-meaning women, this group was working hard to spread the gospel that politics was a dirty business in which women did not belong. The strangeness of a group of women going out of their homes to organize committees aimed at stopping other women from leaving *their* homes never seemed to have struck them.

To counteract such female "anti" activity, the "suffs" had their own surprise affiliate. Harking back to the days when men's anti-slavery and temperance societies had formed female auxiliaries, New York's woman suffragists formed a gentleman's auxiliary. The Men's League for Woman Suffrage was headed by James L. Laidlaw, a respected banker whose wife was one of Mrs. Catt's principal lieutenants. Mr. Laidlaw patiently repeated to newspaper interviewers that "the day of the doll-woman was passing," and that women who voted made far more interesting dinner-table companions than women whose faces turned vacant when politics was mentioned.

Said a headline in the *New York World*: WOMEN BABBLE NO MORE. THEY'VE STOPPED TO THINK, SAYS MALE SUFFRAGETTE.

Mr. Laidlaw and the gentlemen he recruited also marched in the suffrage parades up Fifth Avenue, usually near the end of the line, as a sort of change of pace after spectators had grown used to exclusively female contingents. It was reported that as one parade strode up the avenue, ultraconservative gentlemen leaned out the windows of the Union League Club to watch the sight.

"Schoolteachers!" one club member suddenly gasped to the others watching with him. "I never realized the menace of this movement before! I'll give a hundred dollars to defeat it. Who'll join me?" The clubmen were taking up a collection, when into sight marched Mr. Laidlaw and his cohorts. If looks could have killed, Mr. Laidlaw's whole corps would have dropped that moment. Glorying in their shame, the male suffragists merely laughed and waved to the glowering clubmen.

But the reaction stirred by the parades was increasingly friendly. The change, perhaps at least partly owing to the cessation of outrageous suffrage demonstrations abroad—as a result of the outbreak of the First World War—was reflected in an editorial in the *New York Sun*. Like all but two of the city's ten dailies, the paper had come around to support woman suffrage and it stated:

> The common opinion of unbiased observers in those States where equal suffrage prevails is . . . that the consequences of extending the franchise have been neither so disastrous as the Anti-suffragists predicted, nor so sudden and remarkably beneficial as some enthusiastic reformers expected. . . .
>
> The following points have been pretty well established: (1) Women who have the vote do vote. (2) Their ballot has already passed a considerable body of law. (3) The suffrage States seem to be satisfied to have women go on voting. . . .

If this was a somewhat lukewarm endorsement, the suffrage camp could take consolation. In the closing days of the New Jersey campaign, President Wilson, a resident of that state, finally spoke out.

"I intend to vote for woman suffrage in New Jersey," he said, "because I believe the time has come to extend that privilege to the women of the state . . ."

Had Mr. Wilson stopped at this point, many women would have been better pleased, for the rest of his statement was:

". . . but I shall vote not as the leader of my party in the nation, but only upon my private convictions as a citizen in New Jersey, called upon by the legislature of the state to express my convictions at the polls."

Whether Mr. Wilson's example swayed many of his fellow citizens of New Jersey could not be proved, but 42 per cent of the ballots cast in that state's special October referendum endorsed woman suffrage. It was not enough. The proposition was defeated two weeks before New York, Pennsylvania, and Massachusetts were scheduled to vote. Because the margin by which the women lost in New Jersey was not too overwhelming, Mrs. Catt insisted that with a little extra effort the other states still could be won.

But despite parades and dispassionate reasoning from editorial writers, despite flying squads of suffrage speakers armed with Mrs. Catt's *Twenty-five Answers to Anti's,* despite "tele-suffing" and doorbell-ringing—and despite the affirmative votes of half a million New York men—woman suffrage lost in the Empire State on Election Day of 1915. Seven hundred thousand other men had voted no to it. Half a million additional had not even troubled to vote. The returns from Pennsylvania and Massachusetts were even more discouraging.

A cartoon by the prize-winning Rollin Kirby, printed first in the *New York World* and then reprinted everywhere, summed up the situation pithily. It showed a rough-looking crew of men leaning over their drinks in a saloon while one of them congratulated the others: "Well, Boys, we saved the home!"

There was gloom in New York suffrage headquarters as the trend of the tally became clear. Then Mrs. Catt showed her true mettle. It would take two years for the legal formalities preceding another referendum, but: Out on the street, ladies, she commanded. And the first rally looking toward success in 1917 started then and there, snatching a victory—at least in spirit—right out of the jaws of defeat.

Two
Generals

12

Despite these defeats, 1915 was not a bad year for suffrage. Hundreds of thousands of new recruits committed themselves to the cause that year; mothers, grandmothers, and college girls everywhere awoke each morning with a new sense of purpose. As a result, almost like a smoldering fire suddenly bursting into flame, the American woman suffrage movement took fire in 1916—and Mrs. Catt was drafted to direct a nationwide drive for immediate victory.

There was some friction within the National American Woman Suffrage Association when it became evident that powerful forces wanted Dr. Shaw to step down. Various old-time leaders felt dismay at the whirlwind atmosphere in which they found themselves. But there seemed no stopping the onrush. Mustering a true grace, Dr. Shaw asked her supporters to join her in helping Mrs. Catt. "I realize that my day except for speaking and 'inspiring' has gone by," Dr. Shaw told her friends, "and this is all right. I will speak and 'inspire' my best. I might do worse, I suppose."

Now there was no longer any question whether it was necessary to press for the Anthony amendment. A mass chorus of female voices was clamoring for instant action. But must the state campaigns be dropped?

Certainly not! said Mrs. Catt as she confidently assumed command. Providing the policy line the whole movement had been lacking, she came out strongly for a combined state and federal attack.

By doing so, she unified the movement as it never had been before—and yet, paradoxically, she also guaranteed division in the ranks. This seeming contradiction arose out of the activities of Miss Alice Paul.

After a year or two of comparative calm, Miss Paul and her Washington committee had begun justifying the worst fears of conservative suffragists. By 1914, Miss Paul's committee had renamed itself the Congressional Union, with branches in many states, and it was looking suspiciously like a Pankhurst-style rival to the old established National Suffrage Association. Worse, Miss Paul had begun sounding like Mrs. Pankhurst. In the 1914 Congressional elections, she had taken the same line with regard to the Democratic party that Mrs. Pankhurst had taken toward England's Liberals. The Democrats, said Miss Paul, must make support of woman suffrage a firm plank in the party's platform—or else suffer defeat. When her threat was ignored, she despatched instructions to the voting women of the West. Defeat all Democrats running for Congress, Miss Paul ordered.

Conservative suffragists thought she had lost her mind. Doesn't the woman know the political system in the United States is not the same as the English system? they asked each other. In England it was true, they grudgingly admitted, that Mrs. Pankhurst had had a point. For under the British system, each major party did stand responsible for carrying out a specific program, and the party leadership could be turned out of office if it failed to hold its members in Parliament in line. At any time, a motion of "No confidence" in the government could be proposed, and if it carried, the cabinet had to resign.

In America, party discipline was much weaker. Individual Congressmen could, and frequently did, vote according to their own consciences. On a particular issue it was quite possible for a party platform and the majority of Congressmen in the same party to differ, without causing any governmental crisis. Thus there was no "party responsibility" for suffrage or anything else, as was the case in England.

Furthermore—and here the conservative suffragists could scarcely contain their indignation—to try to defeat all Democrats was lunacy; for some of the staunchest backers of the suffrage cause in Congress happened to be Democrats. Why punish them, and suffrage at the same time, by campaigning against them?

President Wilson was a Democrat and the Democrats had a majority in both houses of Congress, Miss Paul said firmly. They could have put through suffrage if they wanted to. We have to make them want to.

In 1914, only the House of Representatives and part of the Senate had been up for election, and Miss Paul's organization was still young, so the results of her effort had been inconclusive. But in 1916, President Wilson himself was up for re-election, the whole House of Representatives was being replaced, as was a third of the Senate, and Miss Paul's committee had grown into the Woman's Party, a brash and increasingly militant group. The head-shaking it was causing among politicians was probably less, however, than the anguish it was rousing among old-time suffragists.

Miss Paul was giving the whole movement a bad name, they fretted to each other. If she kept up, who knew what might happen? Even good friends of suffrage in Congress and on newspaper editorial pages would surely desert the cause when they saw how dangerously wrong a woman could be about politics. But Mrs. Catt herself did not seem to be much alarmed.

There was no question of her sympathizing with Miss Paul. By her own pronouncements, Mrs. Catt made it plain that she did not like Miss Paul's tactics. Just as piously as any conservative could wish, she condemned the recklessness of trying to defeat good friends of the cause. Yet she probably would not have stopped Miss Paul, even if she could have done so.

For Mrs. Carrie Catt knew politics. A long time ago, a Senator talking about one of his colleagues who was not exactly friendly to suffrage, but not dead set against it either, had said: "He and others will change their minds, not because they see the light, but because they feel the heat." Mrs. Catt understood exactly what the Senator had meant. Let a few lawmakers in suffrage states be defeated by Miss Paul— and then a lot of others would begin feeling less lukewarm.

Already in four years, Miss Paul had done more to make the Anthony amendment a live issue than had been accomplished in the preceding forty years. There was no question of this; even her worst enemies admitted it. Giving in to Miss Paul, and concentrating every drop of energy on the federal campaign, would not do; Mrs. Catt had sound reasons for her conviction on this point. Yet it did no real harm to have a difference of opinion; on the contrary, it probably was all to the good, for the radicals could almost certainly keep stirring calmer souls into continued lively lobbying activity in Washington.

Moderate as well as conservative opinion in the suffrage camp was firmly in favor of the two-pronged campaign Mrs. Catt proposed. Therefore the majority of suffragists loyally followed her, in an impressive display of feminine unity.

On the other hand, the smaller, radical faction could not and would not join the rest because Miss Paul insisted her way was better and would not hear of compromising. So be it, said Mrs. Catt, no doubt with more than a little relief. Having the radicals under her own wing would make for constant squabbling and constant embarrassment before outsiders. With the radicals under their own general, the situation would be different. Embarrassment there might still be, but where a touch of fighting militancy would do the most good, Miss Paul could be counted on to supply it—and Mrs. Catt could appreciate the benefits, meanwhile innocently wringing her hands and telling the newspapers that *her* women would never stoop to such tactics.

Indeed, if the going got rough, and anything like the British window-breaking or mail-burning started, Mrs. Catt could even demonstrate the law-abiding nature of true American womanhood by discreetly letting the authorities know in advance that her spies had reported an outrage was being planned. Gratitude in high places might even repay Mrs. Catt for her trouble.

This in itself was unladylike? Perhaps. But in 1916, the woman suffrage movement took off its white kid gloves and began to play the game of politics in earnest. The moderates, no less than the radicals, were out to win now. If there remained any doubts on this score, they were quickly dispelled by the performance put on when the Presidential election campaign approached.

Ever since Miss Anthony's day, as far back as the 1880's, suffrage delegations had been doggedly showing up when the national conventions of the major parties were writing their platforms. Just as might be expected, the ladies had found no welcome mat out for them when they had appeared to ask for a suffrage plank. Gradually, outright rudeness had given way to courtesy, but the end result had not changed much. Over the years, vague statements to the effect that women deserved well of their country had been included in each party's statement of its aims; that was all. To Mrs. Catt, no less than to Miss Paul, it was no longer enough.

Immediately before the Republican convention opened in Chicago, Miss Paul's new Woman's Party held a convention of its own there. The opening speech by Miss Maud Younger, one of Miss Paul's principal lieutenants, could not but interest Republicans who had already arrived in town. She said:

"For the first time in a Presidential election, voting women are a factor to be reckoned with. Four years ago, women voted in six states—today in twelve, including Illinois. These states with their four million women constitute nearly one-fourth of the Electoral College and more than one-third of the votes necessary to elect a President. With enough women organized in each state to hold the balance of power, the women's votes may determine the Presidency of the United States."

Here was heat indeed. But could Miss Paul really swing any substantial number of votes? Even those men most disposed to laugh off her threat had to stop and wonder, in the face of the cool, competent grasp of political realities demonstrated by this and other speakers.

Mrs. Catt planned her appeal on a different basis, but no less competently. From early February of 1916, she had been "visiting the states" in the manner of a professional politician, conferring everywhere with local leaders of the movement. She told them she wanted a dramatic showing of suffragists from the whole nation when the Republicans met in Chicago in June.

With the unexpected cooperation of the weather, she got even more drama than she had bargained for. It was pouring rain in Chicago on the morning of June 7, the date set by the Republicans for hearings on proposed platform planks. Mrs. Catt had scheduled a parade down Michigan Avenue prior to presenting the request for a suffrage plank, featuring women from every state. According to the plan, the women would march to the Coliseum where the platform hearing was being held, and would, in fact, march right into the hall, to hand in their proposed plank endorsing the Anthony amendment. After that, how could anyone say suffrage was not a mass movement?

But the rain was coming down so hard, and the wind was blowing so fiercely off Lake Michigan, that Mrs. Catt called a meeting in the morning. Already firemen had postponed a parade they had advertised. Mrs. Catt stood up and put the question to her ladies: Should their own parade be called off, and alternate plans be made?

"NO!"

The shouted response clearly pleased her.

"Good!" said Mrs. Catt. "Our parade will start as scheduled, but I advise raincoats and rubbers."

Because elephants were the Republicans' symbol, Mrs. Catt had troubled to hire two elephants to lead the suffrage march. Rubber blankets for the elephants were found; so were umbrellas for the ladies. On schedule, bugles blared into the wind and astounded watchers crowded windows along the route. With two elephants, twenty-four brass bands, a Highland piper and two fife and drum corps, ten thousand women walked briskly down rain-soaked Michigan Avenue.

Inside the Coliseum, a woman representing an anti-suffrage society was testifying. "Women do *not* want the ballot," she was saying. Then suddenly the door swung open. "Don't crowd, ladies!" a policeman bawled. "There are plenty of seats inside! Take your time!" And wave on wave of marchers, dripping wet, their banners sodden, exultantly poured into the auditorium. *Who said women did not want the vote?*

The next morning the *New York Times,* a last-ditch opponent of suffrage on its editorial page, reported on its front page: "CHICAGO July 7—This was no day for men to be out in the cold. The firemen's parade was called off, but 10,000 women took part in the suffrage parade, marching for more than an hour in a heavy downpour and biting wind. . . . Politicians are calling it the pluckiest thing they ever knew women to do. . . ."

But the reward for such valor did not satisfy Mrs. Catt and her marchers. After a private session, which must have been marked by much explosive argument, the Republican platform committee came up with a plank that its chairman, Senator Henry Cabot Lodge of Massachusetts, read out the next day:

"The Republican party, reaffirming its faith in government of the people, by the people and for the people, favors the extension of the suffrage to women—"

Senator Lodge was interrupted here by a burst of cheers from the women in the audience, too elated at the words they had just heard to wait for the rest of the sentence. Smiling frostily, Senator Lodge paused till the cheering died down, then continued:

"BUT we recognize the right of each state to settle this question for itself!"

There was to be no formal Republican support for the Anthony amendment. It was difficult for Mrs. Catt and her colleagues to restrain their disappointment—and yet, what they had got was better than any major party had ever before given the suffrage movement. Besides, there was one more chance this year. Advance guards of Democrats were already assembling in St. Louis for their party's national convention.

Mrs. Catt boarded the next train for St. Louis.

The suffrage demonstration she planned for the Democrats was something new and it made quite an impression. Between the convention hotel in that city and the convention hall, there stretched half a mile of broad boulevard. Every delegate had to travel this route a few times a day, and Mrs. Catt made sure the trip was instructive. Lining both curbs for the entire distance were thousands of women dressed in white with yellow sashes and parasols and state banners over their shoulders. "The Golden Lane," the newspapers immediately tagged the novel suffrage appeal. Indeed the *St. Louis Globe-Democrat* was moved to poetry on the subject, and printed this verse:

> *Citizen and Democrat,*
> *Marching down the Golden Lane*
> *'Neath the eyes of Mrs. Catt,*
> *Marching down the Golden Lane,*
> *Marching out to nominate*
> *Wilson for their candidate—*
> *How the Democrats did hate*
> *Marching down the Golden Lane!*
> *But they couldn't get away*
> *From the "Women's Votes" display.*
> *They'll recall for many a day*
> *Marching down the Golden Lane!*

Running the gauntlet of "The Golden Lane" amused some delegates, unnerved others. Whatever their reaction, though, on one point there could be no disagreement. Mrs. Catt had guaranteed that nobody attending the Democratic National Convention in 1916 would forget that woman suffrage was now a major national issue.

Being traditionally noisier than Republicans, the Democrats put on an uproarious scene right in public when the proposed suffrage plank came up for discussion. On this occasion, "The Golden Lane" had moved en masse to the gallery, from which the ladies listened as various delegations hooted, whistled, and tried to shout down a pro-suffrage Senator.

"Are you *men* that cheer every denunciation of women?" the Senator yelled above the tumult.

Feeling the time had come to help their friend, the ladies in the gallery stood at this moment, unfurling thousands of golden parasols. Waving them and golden banners, they provided a startling picture that took on added impact from thunder and lightning flashes as a sudden storm struck outside the hall.

Within, lobbyists from the brewery trade bustled about the convention floor, openly working to bolster anti-suffrage sentiment. The women could not but note with grim smiles that "The Hidden Enemy" was not hidden here. For several hours, perspiring speakers roared out praise of women who stayed by their firesides, and besought the convention to save the American home and American womanhood from those who wished to destroy family life. What with majority reports and minority reports, the parliamentary situation became enormously confused. But finally a vote—the crucial vote— was announced. Then the women in the gallery whipped out notebooks in which to record the roll call.

Reported the *New York Times:* "The sight of them had a most unnerving effect on the delegations. It was like the French Revolution . . . and the women with the roll call blanks suggested the knitting women of the Reign of Terror. . . ."

Whatever their motivation, when the delegates at last voted, they adopted a suffrage plank not significantly different from the one the Republicans had accepted. "Believing," the Democrats said, "that governments derive their just powers from the consent of the governed, we acknowledge the right of women to participate in government, and favor their enfranchisement." President Wilson himself had approved this wording, and if there was no mention of the federal amendment, at least it put the party squarely in favor of the suffrage principle.

As the *New York Post* said in an editorial: "Woman suffrage has acquired an entirely new status. . . . To have made the conquest over both Republicans and Democrats in a single year is a signal achievement."

Mrs. Catt still was not content, and Miss Paul even less so. In its campaign paper, her Woman's Party said flatly: "The effort of the Woman's Party will be directed toward the defeat of Mr. Wilson and the national Democratic ticket in the twelve equal suffrage states."

The paper went on to explain: "The Woman's Party has been accused of 'being out to punish Mr. Wilson.' They are very indifferent indeed about Mr. Wilson. In thirty-six states they are not attempting to harm a political hair of Mr. Wilson's head. They would view with composure the re-election of Mr. Wilson—but *not* in the equal suffrage states and *not* by the help of the women's votes. One thing we have to teach Mr. Wilson and his party—and all on-looking parties— is that the group which opposes national suffrage for women will lose women's support in twelve great commonwealths controlling nearly a hundred electoral votes; too large a fraction to risk, or to risk twice, even if once risked successfully. If that is made clear, it is a matter of total indifference to the Woman's Party—so far as suffrage is concerned—who is the next President of the United States."

So "General Paul" set out trying to defeat Mr. Wilson and his running mates in the twelve states where women were already voting. And "General Catt" called an emergency suffrage convention for September in Atlantic City, to which she invited both Mr. Wilson and his Republican opponent for the Presidency, Charles Evans Hughes.

Mr. Hughes sent his regrets; unfortunately, the pressure of campaign engagements elsewhere would not permit him to be present. But he also sent along a statement personally endorsing the Anthony amendment. Said the *New York Times* of this unexpected development: "A surprise and a sorrow to many of us."

Needless to say, Mrs. Catt felt quite otherwise. Her main effort in these weeks was directed toward getting President Wilson's promise to come to Atlantic City. In the course of private interviews in the White House, she patiently spread out for him the reports she had received which beyond any possible doubt proved there had been fraud in the count of several state referendums where suffrage had been defeated. Big-city political machines and other unpleasant facts of political life made it extremely unlikely that many states would ever vote for suffrage if left to their own devices, she insisted. Thus, it was morally incumbent on Mr. Wilson to come out in favor of the federal amendment.

Mr. Wilson listened, and withheld decision. His own party was too riddled by anti-prohibition and anti-suffrage elements to make a strong stand plausible, he indicated. But he would think over all she had said. Then, in tribute to her reasoned presentation, he let her take away some hope. Concerning his position, he could make no pledge, but, yes, he *would* come to speak to her women in Atlantic City.

The tension as the emergency conference opened was almost tangible. Never before had a President of the United States addressed a suffrage meeting. How could excitement be contained? Mrs. Catt's own keynote speech caught the mood of the moment.

"The woman's hour has struck!" she started. Then speaking with a mounting urgency, she went on:

> Our movement is like Niagara, a vast volume of water tumbling over its ledge, but turning no wheel. Our machine is set for the propaganda stage, not for the seizure of victory.
>
> If we are to seize victory, there must be a change in mental attitude. THAT CHANGE MUST TAKE PLACE IN THIS HALL, HERE AND NOW!
>
> Women, arise! Demand the vote! The character of a man is measured by his will. The same is true of a movement. Then, will to be free! Demand the vote! WOMEN, ARISE!

And rise they did, in a cheering, shouting, handkerchief-waving mass of determination. Afterward it was an effort to settle down to discuss specific plans until President Wilson should arrive to address them that evening. But somehow they managed to become engrossed.

During the afternoon, Mrs. Catt was tapped on the shoulder and told there was a telephone call for her. As she left the platform, word raced through the hall. The White House wanted her! Was the President not coming, after all?

Mrs. Catt herself was filled with foreboding as she picked up the telephone. But almost instantly, relief lit her face—and she laughed heartily. For the call was from a White House secretary. Mrs. Wilson had decided to accompany the President. And Mrs. Wilson wished to know: what was the proper attire for appearing on the platform at a suffrage meeting?

Still smiling, Mrs. Catt confessed that after many years she herself was not sure if there *was* a proper platform dress. Whatever Mrs. Wilson wore would be appropriate, she added, and with a spring in her step she walked back into the hall to reassure her women.

When President and Mrs. Wilson stepped onto the stage

that evening, the First Lady was wearing a white summer dress, and Mr. Wilson a conventional suit and a solemn air. As the audience rose and cheered him, the President's eyes seemed to travel over the rows of smiling, applauding women, and Mrs. Catt said afterward that a slight smile had made his face suddenly youthful. It was as if at that moment he personally became interested and committed to the suffrage cause, she said.

In his address, he referred to this himself. "I have felt as I sat here tonight the wholesome contagion of the occasion," he said. "Almost every other time that I ever visited Atlantic City, I came to fight somebody. I hardly know how to conduct myself when I have not come to fight anybody, *but with somebody.*"

The applause this remark drew seemed to make him anxious lest his words be misinterpreted. He went on:

> We feel the tide; we rejoice in the strength of it; *and we shall not quarrel in the long run as to the method of it.* Because, when you are working with masses of men and organized bodies of opinion, you have got to carry the organized body along. The whole art and practice of government consists not in moving individuals, but in moving masses. It is all very well to run ahead and beckon, but after all you have got to wait for them to follow.
>
> I have not come to ask you to be patient, because you have been; but I have come to congratulate you that there has been a force behind you that will beyond any peradventure be triumphant, and for which you can a little while afford to wait.

As he concluded, there was applause once more, but the enthusiasm seemed muted. The audience appeared not to know quite what to make of the President's speech. Was it encouraging—or discouraging? Keyed up for something definite, they could not but feel a little disappointed.

Then it was that Dr. Anna Shaw rose from her place on the platform and performed her greatest service to the cause of woman suffrage.

"We have waited long enough, Mr. President, for the vote," she said gently. "We have hoped it might come in your Administration."

In wordless agreement, every woman in that audience rose to her feet, facing Mr. Wilson, with silent appeal written plainly on her face. President Wilson, too, was standing, and preparing to leave for Washington. For a long moment, he and they stood facing each other, and no words were spoken. But still it seemed abundantly clear that something had happened.

Before Mrs. Catt and her women left Atlantic City, they fixed a firm timetable. They would not only pass the Anthony amendment, they decided, but pass it soon. The year 1920 would mark the one hundredth anniversary of Susan B. Anthony's birth. By 1920, they vowed, every woman in the United States would have the right to vote.

The
Power
of
an Idea

=====

13

He kept us out of war!"

It was with this slogan that Woodrow Wilson won re-
election in 1916. The great powers of Europe were engaged
in a war more wide-ranging and more terrible than any the
world had ever known before, and Mr. Wilson's success at
steering a neutral course during the preceding two years un-
doubtedly bulked larger than any other single campaign
issue. Woman suffrage was by no means a decisive factor.

Not that suffrage disappeared from the nation's front
pages. On the contrary, with every passing week the pace of
the movement grew faster, its pressure more intense.

In Miss Paul's camp, there may have been some private dismay over the election results in those states where women
were already voting. No separate tabulation showed how many
women had cast ballots, or whom they had voted for; but the
mere fact that Mr. Wilson owed his slim winning margin to
California and other Western suffrage states gave sufficient
evidence for presuming numerous women voters had failed to
heed the Woman's Party. Instead of voting against Democrats,
women seemed to have been influenced by the peace slogan—
and to have voted in even larger numbers than might have

been expected in favor of Mr. Wilson and his running mates.

Yet if Miss Paul felt discouraged, she did not say so. And she not only claimed her tactics had been responsible for the defeat of several Democratic Congressmen; she also warned she would be coming up with new and even more effective methods in the next few months.

As for Mrs. Catt, she had locked up in her desk a secret document. It was a detailed "Plan of Action," adopted at the emergency convention in Atlantic City after Mr. Wilson's and the reporters' departure. Explicit as a blueprint, this paper gave, step by step, the program to be followed in winning adoption of the Anthony amendment within four years if possible, six years at the very latest. But not a word of this extraordinary document was allowed to appear in print.

What Mrs. Catt had to say publicly was addressed, right after the election, to members of the new Congress.

"Woman suffrage is inevitable—you know it," she told them. Then in the same speech, she added these measured words: "The political parties will go on—we know it. Shall we, then, be enemies or friends? There is one thing mightier than kings or armies, congresses or political parties—*the power of an idea when its time has come to move*. The idea will not perish; the party which opposes it may."

That speech was the signal for the opening of a drive unmatched in all of American history.

Weeks before the new Congress convened, steps had already been taken to ensure that the suffrage amendment would be the first order of business in both houses. There was one new development that made such machinations easier. In the same election which had brought national victory to Mr. Wilson, the voters of Montana had decided to send Miss Jeanette Rankin, former chairman of the state's woman suffrage so-

ciety, to represent them in Washington. Congresswoman
Rankin, needless to say, required no urging to promise she
would introduce the Anthony amendment the instant it was
procedurally possible to do so.

Indeed Miss Rankin's mere arrival in Washington seemed
a happy omen. It even made Miss Paul and Mrs. Catt forget
their differences long enough to sit on either side of the newcomer at a triumphant luncheon honoring the national capital's first feminine lawmaker.

In the Senate, there was no such obvious choice to introduce the bill, but several male Senators chivalrously agreed
to see that suffrage was not bypassed. The behind-scenes
maneuvering responsible for arranging this was largely the
work of a gentle lady from New England who was becoming
one of the most familiar figures on Capitol Hill. Neither an
elected official nor a government employee, she nevertheless
spent every day striding in her neat dark skirt and white
shirtwaist from office to office. She was Mrs. Maud Wood
Park, suffrage lobbyist.

Very soon after the election a handsome sum of money that
had been left to the cause by a rich New Yorker, Mrs. Frank
Leslie, widow of a noted magazine publisher, began at last
to be available for spending. Relatives of Mrs. Leslie had
been contesting her will for several years, but the court
finally decided the lady had had a perfect right to bequeath
her small fortune to Mrs. Catt, to be used "as she shall think
most advisable to the furtherance of the cause of woman's
suffrage." On receiving the first installment, Mrs. Catt used
it to buy a mansion.

The former French Embassy on Rhode Island Avenue in
Washington became Suffrage House. And Suffrage House became the headquarters for one of the most awesome lobbying
operations ever to descend on the national capital.

With the meek-seeming Mrs. Park as the captain in charge,

disciplined companies of suffragists fanned out every morning to call on lawmakers. Unlike some other efforts aimed at
changing legislative minds, there was no secret about what
the ladies were up to; in teasing tribute to the openness of
their effort, Washington observers quickly dubbed it "The
Front Door Lobby."

But if Mrs. Park and her helpers went against lobbying
tradition by avoiding the backstairs routes that were more
usually chosen in this profession, they certainly could not be
dismissed as amateurs. Down to the very finest points, their
drive was organized with an efficiency and precision veteran
political observers had to admit was stunning.

Besides a short course in practical politics, each volunteer
received a written set of rules:

DIRECTIONS FOR LOBBYISTS

  I. Preparation
1. Read our records of each member before calling
   on him. . . .

 II. Interviewing
1. If the member appears busy, ask whether he
   would prefer to see you at some other time.
2. Be courteous no matter what provocation you
   may seem to have to be otherwise.
3. If possible, learn the secretary's name and have
   a little talk with him or her. . . .

And so on, through twelve points defining proper interviewing procedure. Another set of rules directed the making
of reports on each interview:

1. Do not make notes in offices or halls.
2. Do find opportunity to make notes on one interview
   before starting another. If necessary, step into the
   "Ladies" dressing room to do this.
3. Write full report of your interview on the same day
   giving . . .

There then followed seven specific areas of information concerning the suffrage position of each lawmaker, in order that Suffrage House might have whatever facts it wanted right in its own files. Before many weeks had passed, Mrs. Park and her ladies had filled a cabinet with such reports as: "Polite but positive . . . Against woman suffrage—any phase of it . . . Declares that men represent women . . . Has not seen any light at all in progressive legislation."

Or, to Mrs. Park's mind, far more satisfactory was the terse report from the lady who interviewed Representative Fiorello La Guardia, later to be Mayor of New York City. In its entirety, this went: "I'm with you; I'm for it; I'm going to vote for it. Now don't bother me," all spoken in one breath.

Every month or so, a new group of volunteer lobbyists would arrive at Suffrage House to spend as much time as they could spare from their own homes following Mrs. Park's directions up on Capitol Hill. As she became more experienced, Mrs. Park worked out even finer details, establishing, for instance, that at least one lady with a Southern accent must be in each team visiting Southern legislators. She also cheerfully compressed her list of directions into a last-minute list of eight "don'ts," impressed on each new arrival setting out for her first interviewing:

> Don't nag.
> Don't boast.
> Don't threaten.
> Don't lose your temper.
> Don't stay too long.
> Don't talk about your work where you can be overheard.
> Don't give the member interviewed an opportunity to declare himself against the amendment. [This on the grounds that even the most hard-shell "anti" should be

allowed the face-saving factor of not having positively committed himself.]

Don't do anything to close the door to the next advocate of suffrage.

Mrs. Catt and Mrs. Park had no illusions about being able to convert large numbers immediately. They foresaw month on month of effort, which they hoped would have a mounting, cumulative effect. While their "Plan of Action" called for forcing a vote on the amendment as soon as possible, it was their realistic appraisal that passage could not be expected until the next session of Congress, two years hence. Naturally they never admitted this, but private strategy sessions in Suffrage House acknowledged it freely.

How could they be sure the chances for success would be better in two years? The answer to that question lay in Mrs. Catt's locked desk drawer. The secret document prepared in Atlantic City established for the first time in the movement's history that the National Association would be in supreme command. Each cooperating state society pledged itself to follow orders, to embark on a mass campaign to amend its own state's constitution if Mrs. Catt thought such a campaign advisable—and *not* to embark on any such campaign if Mrs. Catt thought to do so would be wasted effort.

Furthermore, Mrs. Catt and her board had outlined a schedule for state referendum campaigns designed to add specific states to the suffrage column, states where there was a good chance of winning and where victory would have important effects on Congress. New York, with the largest single Congressional delegation in Washington, was, for instance, the prime target for 1917.

It had not been easy for Mrs. Catt to win her point that only coordinated state and national action, under national direction, could guarantee success. The old Southern battle

cry of states' rights had sounded once more, and suffrage
societies from the Deep South had refused to go along with
the policy. Nevertheless, Mrs. Catt and her supporters had
triumphed. "Like a well-oiled steam roller," in the words
of one disgruntled Southerner, their forces had pushed
through the program, even securing the grudging assent of
state presidents who would not sign that at the very least they
would not interfere with those who had signed.

Thus Mrs. Catt had what amounted, in plain language, to
a disciplined political machine of her own. Even states which
had already won suffrage for their women were committed
to keep on working—so that at least thirty-six state societies
could plunge into simultaneous campaigns to get their legislatures to ratify the amendment, after it had passed in Congress. But getting two-thirds of the Senate and the House of
Representatives to approve submitting the amendment to
the states was the crucial first step.

Accordingly, once Mr. Wilson was re-elected, the "well-
oiled steam roller" went into action once more, to press state
campaigns in the states Mrs. Catt had chosen, and at the
same time to press increasingly hard in Washington.

Moreover, Miss Paul's followers came up with their own
form of pressure. In January of 1917, groups of sedate young
women, many of them Quakers, began standing outside the
White House gates. They carried signs: "Mr. President, What
Will You Do for Woman Suffrage?" Silently and immovably,
they stationed themselves there every day, in a protest the
likes of which nobody had ever thought of before. Newspapers everywhere printed their pictures. President Wilson
politely tipped his hat to them as he drove through the gates.

Next the young women took to marching back and forth,
instead of merely standing in place in all weather, but still it
seemed no law was being violated. Police let them march on,

Picketing the White House

National Archives

undisturbed. Perhaps this picketing might have gradually ceased attracting any attention—if the atmosphere in Washington had not changed sharply.

In the spring of 1917, war hysteria gripped the city.

By sinking American ships, by taking American lives, Germany aroused the United States to more than anger. Neutrality no longer appeared possible; now the three thousand miles of the Atlantic Ocean no longer provided safety from Europe's fearful upheaval. When the Germans announced their submarines would *not* be ordered to leave American shipping alone, President Wilson felt he had no choice any more. He asked the Congress to declare war.

No matter that suffrage had been promised first place on the legislative agenda; under the circumstances Congresswoman Rankin could do nothing but yield and let the war declaration be debated. In the tense session that followed, Miss Rankin, a convinced pacifist, cast her first vote as a lawmaker—against the prevailing tide. With forty-four male Representatives, she voted against the war declaration.

Amid all the emotions stirred that day, it irked Mrs. Park almost beyond bearing to read in the newspapers that Miss Rankin had wept as she handed in her negative ballot, this being taken by anti-suffragists as proof positive of woman's natural unfitness for the rigors of politics. From her gallery seat, Mrs. Park had had a clear view of the proceedings. Miss Rankin had not shed a tear, Mrs. Park tartly commented, but several men on the House floor had indeed been weeping, both audibly and visibly.

After the war declaration passed, suffrage continued to be shunted aside. By a "gentleman's agreement," the leadership of both houses agreed not to consider any except war measures during this emergency period. Even some dedicated suffragists believed the policy justified. Would it not be unpatriotic to go on with business as usual when American soldiers were preparing to die for their country?

Mrs. Catt rejected this view. Even before the war declaration, when there were unmistakable signs that the crisis was coming closer, she had led her colleagues in adopting a fixed policy. Should war come, the National American Woman Suffrage Association would help the war effort in every possible way, by raising money, by cooperating in efforts to direct women into war industry jobs as men left to put on uniforms. Nevertheless, the Association *would not abandon its fight for suffrage.*

"This is a war to make the world safe for democracy." The words were President Wilson's, and they had stirred a fervor of idealism in England and France as well as the United States. Surely at such a time it would be breaking faith with those who fought if efforts toward improving American democracy were abandoned. So Mrs. Catt reasoned. To a certain extent, Miss Paul agreed.

But in the eyes of Miss Paul and her followers, all war was evil. Mainly from religious conviction, they refused even nominal support of the war effort, and what was more, the ardency of their suffrage convictions led them to put anti-suffragists in the same category as German militarists. President Wilson, by his unwillingness to speak out strongly in favor of the Anthony amendment, by his ignoring the American woman's cries for freedom, was showing himself as hardly any improvement over the German Kaiser, the Woman's Party charged. "Kaiser Wilson," they tauntingly called the President on their picket signs—and that caused trouble in June of 1917.

Soldiers and superpatriots passing the White House became so infuriated that they tore at the signs. Insults were shouted at the women. In the highly emotional climate accompanying the outbreak of war, even peaceful protest against government policy seemed treason to some otherwise reasonable citizens. And so the police broke up the near-riot by arresting not the angry attackers—but the marching women. They were "obstructing the sidewalks," it was held.

No sooner was one group of pickets arrested than another appeared to take their places. Over a period of the next several months, more than two hundred women from twenty-six states were arrested. Ninety-seven of these suffragists landed in prison. Treated as the lowest sort of female offender, they retaliated by going on hunger strikes. At last, Pankhurst militarism had burst into full flower on American shores.

When Its
Time Has Come
to Move

14

War or no war, suffrage gripped the nation's attention. In 1917, the signs were everywhere. After almost seventy years, the idea had finally taken hold; its time had come to move.

In keeping with Mrs. Catt's private timetable, strong local campaigns were mounted during the year by suffrage societies in nine states. One after another, North Dakota, Ohio, Indiana, Rhode Island, Nebraska, Michigan, all succumbed to "the Illinois plan." By the action of each of these legislatures, the referendum route was bypassed, and bills granting women the right to vote for President were adopted. Then Arkansas, in the first suffrage victory in the Deep South, told its women they could vote in primary elections.

Discouraging news did come from Maine, which turned down suffrage in a September referendum. "A battle has been lost," said Mrs. Catt crisply. "Forget it. Others lie ahead." It took no extraordinary insight to realize she was referring first of all to the impending November referendum in New York.

Despite the heartbreaking defeat there two years earlier, the Empire State's united suffrage organizations had swung right back into action. Parades, petitions, the whole paraphernalia of politicking kept the issue boiling. Even without

When this photograph was first printed in 1917, the caption read: "Like ships of the line, suffragettes led by Carrie Chapman Catt parade down Fifth Avenue (in New York) demanding the right to vote."

Courtesy of the New York Historical Society, New York City

Mrs. Catt's personal direction, the drive had a precision and a fervor that called forth the highest form of political compliment.

"If you can't beat 'em, join 'em!" That was the standard rule for big-city political machines—and in the autumn of 1917, New York's Tammany Hall heeded it. Having concluded that suffrage could not be beaten, Tammany decided to stop trying. Since a good many wives and daughters of these Democratic gentlemen were openly marching in suffrage parades on Fifth Avenue, the decision by the machine's powers must have restored political peace in numerous families. It also supplied just the touch necessary for bringing the great state of New York into the suffrage column. After November of 1917, New York's women had the vote, and the biggest Congressional delegation in Washington, and the biggest bloc of power in choosing a President, could no longer ignore the wishes of the women of the state.

Such a change was exactly what Mrs. Catt had calculated on. To use the added strength of each additional suffrage state as an additional lever in pressing for adoption of the Anthony amendment—that was the crux of Mrs. Catt's strategy. Her basic quarrel with Miss Paul lay in the latter's insistence that state campaigns did not really matter. Oh, indeed they did! In January of 1918, just two months after New York went for suffrage, the House of Representatives in Washington put aside war business to take a historic vote.

Only once before, in 1915, had suffrage reached the voting stage in the House. Then the proposition that the Anthony amendment should be submitted to the several states had won a majority vote, but did not carry; on such questions, a full two-thirds affirmative tally was required.

Had any playwright invented the scene that occurred when the second suffrage vote was scheduled three years later, he would surely have been accused of exaggerating. To begin with, Mrs. Park and her lobbyists had gone over and over their reports. It seemed incredible—and yet *exactly the required two-thirds had signified they would vote aye.* If a single supporter changed his mind, the resolution would be lost. Amid breathless suspense, the count started. Then in one emotion-packed episode after another, the fact that suffrage was no longer merely a woman's crusade became ever clearer.

A Tennessee Representative who had just broken his arm and shoulder refused to go into a hospital to have the bones set; despite great pain, he insisted on voting for suffrage first. An Illinois Republican left the hospital where he had been confined during the past six months; so weak his voice could hardly be heard, he spoke up for suffrage. A New Yorker left his dying wife's bedside—to keep his promise to her, he said—and voted for suffrage. In fact, only four from New York's delegation of more than forty failed to vote for suffrage. In all, fifty-six men who had said nay to suffrage three years earlier changed their stand. Thus on January 10, 1918, by a vote of 274 to 136—exactly the necessary two-thirds margin—the House of Representatives endorsed the Anthony amendment.

As the result became clear, after three separate roll calls to make sure there had been no error, a woman's voice rose from one of the corridors in reverent song: "Praise God from whom all blessings flow . . ." Then from the galleries, from the floor itself, other voices, women's voices and men's voices, joined in the hymn "Old Hundred," producing a spontaneous chorus that those present would never forget.

By a remarkable coincidence, on this very same day, three thousand miles away in London, Britain's House of Lords also voted in favor of woman suffrage. The House of Commons there had already given in, and so the battle was won in Britain. But victory in the United States had not yet been assured. There was still the Senate to convince—and then the legislatures of at least thirty-six states.

Nevertheless, Mrs. Catt issued a jubilant statement: "The women of America will be voters in 1920, the one hundredth anniversary of the birth of Susan B. Anthony." No longer was her timetable a secret. Her words appeared in newspapers all over the country, and for the moment, suffrage chased even the war news from France out of the top headlines.

As a result, Mrs. Catt made what was, for her, a rash decision. She ordered a new dress, to be worn on a special set of occasions; it was to be the mainstay of her wardrobe on the "ratification tour" she intended taking right after the Senate acted, to spur state suffrage societies into pressing state legislatures for immediate approval of the amendment. Unhappily, Mrs. Catt's dress would no longer be new by the time she could begin her tour. "You can't hustle the Senate," veteran Washington observers warned her. They were not mistaken.

After the House acted, the suffrage lobby concentrated its full force on the Senate. But although there were fewer Senators to convince, Senators notoriously resisted changing their minds. By Suffrage House count, the cause was still two votes short of a two-thirds margin in the Senate—and winning those two votes proved infuriatingly difficult.

Since the rules of the Senate gave ample leeway to those preferring delay, it was September of 1918 before the subject even came up for debate. Realizing the scope of the problem by this time, Mrs. Catt had adjusted her tactics to place great emphasis on getting President Wilson to speak publicly in favor of action by the Senate. But throughout the summer, Mr. Wilson put her off because the war overseas had reached a crucial period. The Germans had attacked in July and been beaten back; the armies of the United States, Britain, and France were surging ahead; the prospect of victory and the problems of arranging peace occupied him increasingly. Still, at the end of September, when the Senate at last was considering suffrage, Mr. Wilson finally gave the matter his attention.

First he privately asked several Senators to vote for the amendment. Then, after so long and gradual a process of changing his own mind, President Wilson dramatically staked his personal prestige on securing Senate approval for suffrage. In a startling departure from tradition, he drove down Pennsylvania Avenue to plead from the Senate rostrum for passage of the measure under debate.

"I tell you plainly," Mr. Wilson told a hushed Senate, "that this measure which I urge upon you is vital to the winning of the war. . . . And not to the winning of the war only. It is vital to the right solution of the great problems which we must settle, and settle immediately, when the war is over."

In short, American democracy must prove its high purpose by granting its women full citizenship. And the women of America must have a voice in deciding the terms of the peace. But as strongly as Mr. Wilson put these points, they still made slight impression on the Senate. No sooner had the President gathered up his manuscript and gone back to the White House, when a Missouri Senator stood up and shouted sarcastically: "A petticoat brigade awaits outside, and Senate leaders like pages trek back and forth for orders!"

Then up jumped a South Carolinian. Instead of praising pure womanhood and denouncing agitators out to destroy the home, the usual Southern anti-suffrage tactic in Senate debate, he openly voiced the real reason for the last-ditch Southern opposition:

"I warn every man here today that when the test comes, as it will come, when the clamor for Negro rights shall have come, that you Senators from the South voting for [woman suffrage] have started it here this day. . . ."

But not only racial prejudice was involved in the bitter anti-suffrage campaign in the Senate. There was an "unholy alliance," Mrs. Catt said grimly, between the Southern racists and a group of die-hard conservatives from Northern industrial states. It was melodramatic to hiss that these Senators were "in the pay of the interests," yet there seemed some truth in the charge.

Various powerful businessmen had come to hate and fear any government regulation of their free-wheeling ways with such a passion that the mere possibility that women would tend to support reform legislation caused them to spend large sums fighting suffrage. Whether any Senators actually received any of this money was never proved; possibly the Senators involved were merely unpaid spokesmen for the business interests they supported. However, there was some evidence that anti-suffrage propaganda of many sorts was paid for from the treasuries of big business.

Ironically, in these months the liquor industry was no longer suffrage's main enemy. Prohibition on a national scale had already been approved by Congress a year before; too late, the liquor industry had discovered that the Southern "Bible belt," where woman suffrage had little appeal, was the real danger to its future.

If the prohibitionists had had an easy time of winning votes from Southern Senators, the suffragists could hardly have fared worse. The day after President Wilson spoke to the Senate, that august body voted; and the tally stood just where Mrs. Park and her lobbyists had gloomily reported it would. Sixty-two Senators had voted for the amendment, only thirty-four against it; but this was still two votes short of the necessary two-thirds. And the South still stood almost solidly against suffrage.

The Senate had voted on October 1, 1918, only a month before another national election. If there remained any lingering feeling that Mrs. Catt was too ladylike in her tactics, her next move dispelled it. With cold political logic, she picked four anti-suffrage Senators who were up for re-election in states in which women could cast ballots. Defeat these four, she ordered.

Perhaps the fragile Alice Paul, who had been called unwomanly and worse some years earlier when she had suggested such action, was now wryly amused by Mrs. Catt's conversion. If so, she failed to comment publicly; she was too busy striding in and out of jail as a result of White House picketing episodes.

Thus, while her Woman's Party kept applying pressure of the most militant sort, Mrs. Catt's moderates calmly took on the task of punishing lawmakers at the polls. And when the vote was counted, two out of the four selected Senators had lost their seats. In addition, in the same election, South Dakota, Michigan, and Oklahoma gave their women full suffrage; even the Southern state of Louisiana came within a few thousand votes of accepting the proposed reform.

Now there could be not a shred of doubt. Suffrage would win the Senate in the next Congress.

But for tactical reasons, it seemed wise to try another vote before the new Congress took its seats. Because many state legislatures met only in alternate years, the process of obtaining sufficient ratifications before 1920 would be extremely difficult if Senate approval of the Anthony amendment could not be secured until after the late spring of 1919. The old Congress would continue meeting for another several months; was it not possible that the clear popular mandate suffrage had just received would change two Senatorial minds?

Possible it may have been, but it did not happen. Once more, in February of 1919, the outgoing Senate voted down suffrage.

In May of 1919, when the next Congress met, there was no crackle of high drama. Almost methodically, the new House of Representatives went through the motions of approving the Anthony amendment, this time with forty-two votes to spare and no emotional hymn-singing after the tally was completed.

Even in the Senate, the debate was almost listless, for the result of the voting was a foregone conclusion. On June 4, 1919, sixty-six United States Senators voted for woman suffrage. By exactly the required margin, the Nineteenth Amendment to the Constitution would now be sent to the several states for ratifying.

If Senate approval was after all virtually an anticlimax, there was still excitement to come. Mrs. Catt was determined to keep to the 1920 deadline, and that meant state after state would have to be swayed to call lawmakers for a special legislative session. A new dress for her ratification tour was now the last thing on Mrs. Catt's mind. Instead she had a small black "ratification notebook"—and on that she put hours of work.

Immediately after the Senate acted, she telegraphed every governor to ask the promptest possible action on ratification. The replies, or lack of same, were then jotted in the notebook, as was every scrap of information pertinent to the prospects for quick approval of the amendment. There were a few pages for each of the forty-eight states, listing key individuals to be called on for help and cryptic comments about the probable legislative decision in each capital.

Despite Mrs. Catt's enormous fund of information, and regardless of her careful planning, even she was surprised by the sequence of ratifications. Wyoming, which had been the first suffrage territory in the nation, might have been expected to be among the first to ratify; instead that honor went to Wisconsin, within the same week the Senate acted in Washington. That week, Illinois and Michigan also formally approved the amendment.

From then on progress was slow, sometimes discouragingly so. When one governor after another protested that there were no funds in the state treasury to pay for a special session, Mrs. Catt whipped up enthusiasm among state suffrage societies for a money-saving scheme. Not only should individual legislators be appealed to, to give a few days of their time without any extra pay as a patriotic duty, she suggested; but also dedicated suffragists could do one last service for the cause by volunteering to serve as unpaid clerks and pages. Never had Mrs. Catt's wisdom in refusing to let state societies disband right after their own state approved suffrage seemed more farsighted than it did during the summer of 1919, when urgent drives to speed the ratifying procedure had to be undertaken in state after state.

Thirty-six states had to ratify, and by September only thirteen had acted. Wyoming at last came through, in January of 1920; it was number twenty-seven. On March 22, the state of Washington moved into line, becoming number thirty-five. Then tension reached the acute stage. Which state could possibly be counted on to make thirty-six?

In her private notes, Mrs. Catt wrote frankly: "I count that Maryland, Virginia, North Carolina, South Carolina, Florida, Georgia, Alabama, Mississippi, Louisiana, and Delaware will not ratify, at least the first year. If the opposition could hold Pennsylvania and New Jersey, and one other state in addition to these ten, we would be beaten on ratification. . . ."

Tennessee proved the crucial arena. When the governor of that state called a special session to convene on August 9 for a vote on the amendment, an emergency summons went up to Washington from the Tennessee suffrage chairman. Come at once, she wired Mrs. Catt. Packing an overnight bag, Mrs. Catt journeyed southward, expecting to spend only a few days away from her office. Instead she stayed two months.

A situation as bizarre as any in American history developed in the capital of Tennessee when that special session convened. Despite the weight of logic and the loss of various court cases, the "anti's" had far from given up. At the very least, they hoped a delaying action would prevent women from voting on a nationwide basis in the Presidential election coming in November; and at best, from their point of view, there still remained some possibility that further court action could stop ratification for good and all. Thus a strange and awesome assortment of "anti's" converged on Nashville to try to hold the line there.

In the very hotel where Mrs. Catt was staying, various private rooms were booked for unidentified parties. Members of the Tennessee legislature seemed to come and go in response to mysterious invitations. On entering the private rooms, the legislators appeared normally sober, but on departing, their gait could only be described as unsteady.

Writing about the experience later, Mrs. Catt noted: "Tennessee had been a prohibition state before the Eighteenth Amendment was submitted, and the state had also ratified that amendment. Why was not the law enforced? asked the women. 'Now see here,' was the reply, 'in Tennessee whiskey and legislation go hand in hand.' "

If the women would not ply the legislators with liquor, they were prepared to use every legitimate means of persuasion. In addition to Mrs. Catt and her lobbyists, there were experienced workers from the Woman's Party on hand. Informally, yet amicably, now that final victory seemed almost within grasp, the two suffrage camps cooperated on seeking vote pledges.

As one hectic day succeeded the next, it became plain that the result of the tally was going to be extremely close. Indeed there seemed a good possibility that the question of whether or not Tennessee would ratify, and whether or not the women of America would cast ballots in November, might well hinge on the switching of a single vote in Nashville.

Then just at the critical moment, the aged Mrs. J. L. Burn from up in the mountains of east Tennessee wrote to her son Harry, who had left home to be a lawmaker. She had been distressed at what she had read in the local news about Harry's failure to make up his mind. She wrote:

> Dear Son:
>   Hurrah and vote for suffrage! Don't keep them in doubt. I notice some of the speeches against. They were bitter. I have been watching to see how you stood, but have not noticed anything yet. Don't forget to be a good boy and help Mrs. Catt put "rat" in ratification.
>   Your Mother

And when the roll was finally called in Nashville, Harry Burn spoke up loud and clear. "Aye!" he voted, to please his old mother.

The vote was a betrayal in the eyes of "anti's," for Mr. Burn had already promised to vote against suffrage. To explain his change in position, he produced his mother's letter.

Then cries of anguish rose over Nashville, and ugly reports of fraud circulated. Mr. Burn had allowed his vote to be bought, it was charged, and the alleged letter was a fake to mask the trickery in a mantle of mother love. Demands for a recount were shouted. While the nation held its breath waiting to see what would happen next in Tennessee, Mrs. Burn wrote once more from up in the mountains:

> Woman was here today, claims to be wife of Governor of Louisiana and secured an interview with me and tried by every means to get me to refute and say that the letter I sent to my son was false. . . . This woman

was very insulting to me in my home and I had a hard
time to get her out of my home. . . .

For all practical purposes, that message settled the issue.
Despite some threats and some new efforts to throw the whole
question back into the courts, the affirmative vote of the
Tennessee legislature was allowed to stand. In Washington,
formal notice that thirty-six states had now ratified was trans-
mitted to the Secretary of State. Then upon the completion
of a few simple legal formalities, the Nineteenth Amendment
to the United States Constitution was declared the law of the
land. Before the end of August, the women of America
flocked to register in order to vote in the Presidential election
of 1920 in November.

One of these women had a moving story to tell interviewers. In upstate New York, Mrs. Charlotte Woodward had
passed her ninetieth birthday. She was the only living person
who remembered the summer day back in 1848, when she
and other farm girls had driven into town to hear Mrs.
Elizabeth Cady Stanton. Said Mrs. Woodward in 1920:

> I do clearly remember the wonderful beauty of the
> early morning when we dropped all our alloted tasks
> and climbed into the family wagon to drive over the
> rough roads to Seneca Falls. At first we traveled quite
> alone under the overhanging tree branches and wild
> vines, but before we had gone many miles we came on
> other wagonloads of women, bound in the same direc-
> tion. As we reached different crossroads, we saw wagons
> coming from every part of the county, and long before
> we reached Seneca Falls we were a procession. . . .

In 1920, that procession finally reached its destination. By
law, the women of America had won full citizenship. How
would they use their new power?

A
Parting
Debate

===

15

How have women used their new power?

Nearly fifty years later, it is still not easy to answer that question. Almost everywhere on the earth, women have gained the rights Mrs. Elizabeth Cady Stanton fought for, and when, in 1966, the vast subcontinent of India chose a woman as Prime Minister, surely Mrs. Stanton's spirit must have rejoiced. But aside from such special cases, has the legal emancipation of women significantly changed the course of recent history?

In the United States, neither politicians nor professors can say positively.

Politicians as a group pride themselves on being hard-headed realists, and by and large they minimize women's contribution. Professors, on the other hand, tend to take a broader view. Thus an imaginary debate between a party chairman and a teacher of political science might prove helpful in clarifying the issue.

"Sure, the ladies have cleaned up a few bad local situations here and there," the politician concedes in his opening statement. "But when it comes to national policy, women don't have anything like the influence some people thought they might have."

"Not so," the professor argues. "Merely because women have not voted as women, but as citizens, it's impossible to write off their effect on policy. Just as should have been expected, it turns out there are women Democrats and women Republicans. There is no 'woman's vote' as such, but women voters, along with their husbands and brothers, quite emphatically express their opinions at the polls."

"Ha!" chuckles the politician. "You mean, they express their emotions. The only real change they've brought about is that they've made it impossible for a man who doesn't appeal to the ladies to get elected President."

"Again not so," retorts the professor. "If you need a villain, it's television. When you have candidates coming into everybody's living rooms, naturally a man with a cold, unpleasing personality isn't going to be welcomed. If you think women are more likely to be taken in by a rabble-rouser, or a fake of any sort, just look back on some of the candidates, both local and national, who succeeded in getting elected before 1920."

Although the politician is far from convinced, he is willing to change course and offer a different argument.

"You have to admit," he says, "the ladies really aren't interested in politics. What better proof is there than the fact that they don't go out and work at it? A very small minority of well-dressed matrons joins the League of Women Voters and studies water pollution and such issues. No doubt they have some effect on local city councils. But when it comes to party politics, where the power is, the ladies are too delicate to dirty their hands, and so they're on the outside. Of one hundred United States Senators, how many are women? One or two! If women had a gift for politics, about half the Senate would be female."

"You've a lot of complicated problems tangled up there," the professor says patiently. "On the matter of women winning what would seem to be their fair share of public offices, I'll grant you that in this country they don't have anything like what would be a proportional representation, although in various other countries as unlike as England and Japan the situation is different. But why don't we have more women Senators? It seems to me there are two underlying reasons."

"That so?"

"In the first place," the professor goes on calmly, "our society still shows more than a slight, lingering prejudice against women entering politics. I'm sure nobody seriously thinks women should not have the vote, after all, but a lot of men still think it's 'unwomanly' if their wives speak up during a political discussion in a living room, let alone an auditorium. Many girls are brought up to think the same way. But a good many intelligent females do turn up at party committee meetings—and then they're usually treated as merely well-meaning amateurs. When it comes to stuffing envelopes with party literature, or other such routine chores, they're in great demand. But when the time arrives for setting policy, or picking candidates, the men don't really want them around."

The politician grins a bit sheepishly, but remains silent.

Warming to his subject, the professor continues: "Since 1920, in fact, only one woman—Mrs. Eleanor Roosevelt—has succeeded in winning a place in the inner councils of a political party. Even before her husband became President, he encouraged her to do some of the politicking he couldn't manage after he got polio. Then she acquired so much influence in her own right that when he died she was still sought out by candidates who wanted her support. Incidentally, do you happen to know the most practical way for a woman to get ahead in the world of politics?"

"What's that?"

"She ought to marry a man with a political following, and if you'll forgive my adopting your own cynical tone for a minute, she ought to hope her husband will not live too long. Then she has a good chance of succeeding him. More often than most people realize, this has been the way a woman has won a major party nomination. Then, once she's been elected on what you might call sentimental grounds, if she does a good job it's hard to ignore her claims, and she may be repeatedly nominated."

"Interesting," says the politician grudgingly. "But that's certainly not the whole story. If more women really wanted to run for office, they'd do it. I still say most of them are just plain not interested enough and not capable enough—"

"You bring me to my second reason," the professor interrupts. "You must agree that there are some women who have served in Congress with distinction, and many more who've done splendidly at the hard job of organizing local political campaigns. But politics is a demanding business, one of the most demanding. And there are many subtle influences in our culture that keep women from a more active role in politics. Nobody tells men who want to run for public office that they mustn't get married and raise a family; as a matter of fact, a bachelor is not considered a good candidate, and a man running for election is expected to have a smiling wife at his side. For a woman, though, the situation is quite different. As our society is presently constituted, most women cannot give up the time—or the money to pay baby sitters— that active participation in politics takes. Unless they are spinsters or widows, they have family responsibilities which they cannot shirk."

"There we have it!" the politician exclaims triumphantly. "Now weren't the 'anti's' right? Isn't a woman's place in her own home?"

"But times are changing," the professor replies mildly.

"More women than ever before *are* working at jobs outside their homes. Whether anybody likes it or not, the old pattern *is* changing. And perhaps new ways will be found to make it possible for women with an interest in politics and a gift for politics to make their contribution, without having to sacrifice the happiness of becoming wives and mothers."

The politician shakes his head wordlessly, and then shrugs. "One thing you will admit," he concludes, "you will have to admit that amending the Constitution really does not produce any magic effect on human nature."

And the professor nods. For indeed the Nineteenth Amendment of itself has not, in nearly fifty years, wrought great changes in America—any more than enacting new civil rights laws can stamp out overnight the injustices suffered by Negro citizens. It is not easy to modify old patterns. But if the struggle for greater human freedom still goes on, surely Lucretia Mott would not be discouraged. She would gently point out that much progress has been made since her day, and thus it must be possible that even further advances can be anticipated in the years to come, if only those who cherish freedom will keep on striving to achieve a more nearly perfect democracy.

Declaration of Sentiments Adopted at Seneca Falls

The following is the text of the declaration adopted at the historic woman's rights convention at Seneca Falls, New York, on July 20, 1848:

DECLARATION OF SENTIMENTS

When, in the course of human events, it becomes necessary for one portion of the family of man to assume among the people of the earth a position different from that which they have hitherto occupied, but one to which the laws of nature and of nature's God entitle them, a decent respect to the opinions of mankind requires that they should declare the causes that impel them to such a course.

We hold these truths to be self-evident: that all men and women are created equal; that they are endowed by their Creator with certain inalienable rights; that among these are life, liberty, and the pursuit of happiness; that to secure these rights governments are instituted, deriving their just powers from the consent of the governed. Whenever any form of government becomes destructive of these ends, it is the right of those who suffer from it to refuse allegiance to it, and to insist upon the institution of a new government, laying its foundation on such principles, and organizing its powers in such form, as to them shall seem most likely to effect their safety and happiness. Prudence, indeed, will dictate that governments long established should not be changed for light and transient causes; and accordingly all experience hath shown that mankind are more disposed to suffer, while evils are sufferable, than to right themselves by abolishing the forms to which they were accustomed. But when a long train of abuses and usurpations, pursuing invariably the same object, evinces a design to˙reduce them under absolute despotism, it is their duty to throw off such government, and to provide new guards for their future security. Such has been the patient sufferance of the women under this government, and such is now the necessity which constrains them to demand the equal station to which they are entitled.

The history of mankind is a history of repeated injuries and usurpations on the part of man toward woman, having in direct object the establishment of an absolute tyranny over her. To prove this, let facts be submitted to a candid world.

He has never permitted her to exercise her inalienable right to the elective franchise.

He has compelled her to submit to laws, in the formation of which she had no voice.

He has withheld from her rights which are given to the most ignorant and degraded men—both natives and foreigners.

Having deprived her of this first right of a citizen, the elective franchise, thereby leaving her without representation in the halls of legislation, he has oppressed her on all sides.

He has made her, if married, in the eye of the law, civilly dead.

He has taken from her all right in property, even to the wages she earns.

He has made her, morally, an irresponsible being, as she can commit many crimes with impunity, provided they be done in the presence of her husband. In the covenant of marriage, she is compelled to promise obedience to her husband, he becoming to all intents and purposes her master—the law giving him power to deprive her of her liberty and to administer chastisement.

He has so framed the laws of divorce, as to what shall be the proper causes, and in case of separation, to whom the guardianship of the children shall be given, as to be wholly regardless of the happiness of women—the law, in all cases, going upon a false supposition of the supremacy of man, and giving all power into his hands.

After depriving her of all rights as a married woman, if single, and the owner of property, he has taxed her to support a government which recognizes her only when her property can be made profitable to it.

He has monopolized nearly all the profitable employments, and from those she is permitted to follow, she receives but a scanty remuneration. He closes against her all the avenues to wealth and distinction which he considers most honorable to himself. As a teacher of theology, medicine, or law, she is not known.

He has denied her the facilities for obtaining a thorough education, all colleges being closed against her.

He allows her in Church, as well as State, but a subordinate position, claiming Apostolic authority for her exclusion from the ministry, and, with some exceptions, from any public participation in the affairs of the Church.

He has created a false public sentiment by giving to the world a different code of morals for men and women, by

which moral delinquencies which exclude women from society are not only tolerated, but deemed of little account
in man.

He has usurped the prerogative of Jehovah himself, claiming it as his right to assign for her a sphere of action, when
that belongs to her conscience and to her God.

He has endeavored, in every way that he could, to destroy
her confidence in her own powers, to lessen her self-respect,
and to make her willing to lead a dependent and abject life.

Now, in view of this entire disfranchisement of one-half
the people of this country, their social and religious degradation—in view of the unjust laws above mentioned, and because women do feel themselves aggrieved, oppressed, and
fraudulently deprived of their most sacred rights, we insist
that they have immediate admission to all the rights and
privileges which belong to them as citizens of the United
States.

In entering upon the great work before us, we anticipate
no small amount of misconception, misrepresentation, and
ridicule; but we shall use every instrumentality within our
power to effect our object. We shall employ agents, circulate
tracts, petition the State and National legislatures, and en-
deavor to enlist the pulpit and the press in our behalf. We
hope this Convention will be followed by a series of Conventions embracing every part of the country.

Bibliography

Blackwell, Alice Stone, *Lucy Stone, Pioneer Woman Suffragist*. Boston: Little Brown, 1930.

Blatch, Harriot Stanton, and Lutz, Alma, *Challenging Years*. New York: Putnam's, 1940.

Cromwell, Otelia, *Lucretia Mott*. Cambridge: Harvard University Press, 1958.

Dorr, Rheta Child, *Susan B. Anthony*. New York: Frederick A. Stokes, 1928.

Flexner, Eleanor, *Century of Struggle*. Cambridge: Belknap Press of Harvard University Press, 1959.

Hallowell, Anna Davis, Editor, *James and Lucretia Mott: Life and Letters*. Boston, 1884.

Irwin, Inez Haynes, *The Story of the Woman's Party*. New York: Harcourt Brace, 1921.

Lutz, Alma, *Susan B. Anthony*. Boston: Beacon Press, 1959.

Nye, Russel B., *William Lloyd Garrison and the Humanitarian Reformers*. Boston: Little Brown, 1955.

Pankhurst, Emmeline, *My Own Story*. New York, 1914.

Park, Maud Wood, *Front Door Lobby*. Boston: Beacon Press, 1960.

Peck, Mary Gray, *Carrie Chapman Catt*. New York: H. W. Wilson, 1944.

Sinclair, Andrew, *The Better Half*. New York: Harper & Row, 1965.

Stanton, E. C., *Eighty Years and More*. New York, 1898.

Stanton, Theodore, and Blatch, Harriot Stanton, Editors, *Elizabeth Cady Stanton as Revealed in Her Letters, Diary and Reminiscences*, 2 vols. New York: Harper, 1922.

Thomas, John L., *The Liberator: William Lloyd Garrison*. Boston: Little Brown, 1963.

The main sources for this book have been diaries, memoirs, old newspapers. Much material that might otherwise have been lost was collected during the 1880's by Mrs. Stanton, Miss Anthony, and various associates, and then embodied in a monumental *History of Woman Suffrage,* which was privately printed; that has been invaluable to me, for it included copies of speeches and programs of meetings as well as a treasury of firsthand recollections by dozens of leading participants in the suffrage struggle. Various individual memoirs published in the nineteenth century and available only in specialized libraries also were most helpful. As for the early twentieth century, the Backus collection of scrapbooks in the New York Historical Society and various scrapbooks in the Library of Congress provided much anecdote material. The above bibliography has, however, been limited to books that are widely available in public libraries and that may have some interest for younger readers.

D.F.

Index